MULTIPLE STREAMS OF INCOME

Because Living Off of One Paycheck Isn't Working Anymore

Special Thanks

We generously thank our graphics team and Jessica Godbee, who assisted with flyers and promotions. Thank you Mr. and Mrs. Roach for making our incredible cover. And we extend much appreciation to each and every member of our publishing team at Show Your Success Publishing. Thank you Angela Sims for your incredible work with our book launch. We also thank all the customers who pre-ordered books. Your name and information, if given, is included in the chapter of the author you supported.

Table of Contents

Foreword

Have you ever observed something simple in appearance, but intriguing once you consider its function and purpose? Like the switch that connects you with light, the "enter" key that connects you with a world of information and engagement, or the lock that connects you with a sense of security? All of these things attach themselves to a greater intent, much more significant but not independent of the smaller objects. Similar to these examples is the concept of multiple streams of income. Each stream of income connects to a greater body which serves an ultimate purpose. Know that every purpose is going to be different for every person or group. Whether that purpose is a program for inmates to reconnect with families, helping small business owners succeed in their markets, or helping children in an underdeveloped area, the multiple streams simply serve as sources of support. This is why we value those who have an understanding of what seems to be a simple principle and are willing to share their insight in a practical way.

We often hear people say the reason for multiple streams of income is to ensure security in case one stops or slows down. This is only partially true. Looking at it from this perspective forces you to focus on and prepare for the things that you don't want to happen instead of the favorable things that you do want to happen. Multiple streams create energy – a surge that allows the larger pool to mature and flow more freely. Imagine how liberating it was for us to learn this. We were a young couple, barely married a year when we had a paradigm shift. To learn that we no longer had to be at the mercy of our physical abilities to work and focus on one or two streams of income just to sustain immediate responsibilities showed that we are graced with a much different type of power—the power to create. We were living off of the many misconstrued catchphrases about money, and we had to solidly start on a new financial path of understanding the importance of creating multiple streams of income.

Getting insight from this collection of authors and professionals within a number of fields serves as a catalyst for service. To have such a resource is invaluable. Creating multiple streams of income, like a stream of water, will encounter some rough terrain as it progresses from its point of origin to the larger body it flows to. But once the path is cleared, the flow becomes natural, just as your regard to the light switch, the enter key, or the lock on your door. They are necessary to connect to a greater source, and stronger collectively to serve a greater purpose.

—James and Natasha Roach, Owners of M & MR Marketing, LLC

Introduction

These times are the best times to become an entrepreneur. The cost of living is increasing while jobs are decreasing. Technology is replacing many labor jobs that we built this world on, and we have more talented individuals willing to work for far less than many top paying jobs used to pay. There are so many college graduates who are not able to find a job in their degree and have had to move back in with their parents.

While becoming an entrepreneur takes focus as well as daily commitments, when all is said and done, there is nothing like having your own business. This book is designed to show you how to be a part of an industry working for yourself and making a full-time income. The authors in this book have been able to make at least what is considered to be the average income in a 12-month time period working in their respective industries. With this book, you will be able to make a decision on which industry would be a better fit for you. You will be able to have direct connection with any of the authors you choose. The purpose is to show you that there are simply *too many ways to make money.*

Building multiple streams of income is no longer a luxury; it has become a necessity. If the high rate of unemployment and mounting job losses have taught us anything, it is that nobody's job is safe. Unfortunately for most people, their only source of income is from their job, which can be a risky way to live. Some couples may be more fortunate and have a spouse bringing in money each month, but they are still relying on a job for their livelihood.

Because of the financial risks involved with relying on a job for all of your incoming cash, it is critical to consider having at least one additional source of income. The list below details a few reasons why having several sources of money coming in is important and how this extra cash can be used.

Here are ten simple reasons why building multiple income streams is so important. Each item listed below is an example of how alternative income sources can be used to lessen the risk of living on a single income.

1. **Rising Health Care Costs** – Whether you are in favor of the health care reform or not, chances are you are feeling the nice increase of higher health care costs. Adding an extra income source can go a long way in paying for things like rising prescription costs and unexpected medical costs.

2. **Unemployment** – How safe is your job? Let's face it, no job is really ever safe, especially in a tough economy. Having other sources of income can help you deal with a job loss much easier than being caught off guard. Even if your other sources of cash can't cover all of your monthly expenses, it can still give you time to figure things out.

3. **Paying for College** – How much are you saving for your kid's college education? Instead of putting your retirement at risk by saving up for your child's secondary education, why not create an alternative income stream to help out? Having multiple streams of income bringing in cash every month can help ease the burden of paying for college.

4. **Living Within Your Means** – In order to build true wealth, you must be able to live within your means. If it is impossible to cut your spending any further, or you just don't want to sacrifice anymore—create a new source of money. I learned this quickly; we don't have to cut back, we just have to learn more ways to increase our bottom line. There are only two ways to live within your means—either spend less or make more money.

5. **Pay Cash for Purchases** – How many times have you been able to pay cash for a car or could pay for a large home improvement project without taking out a loan? A second or third income stream could be used to save for these types of purchases so you don't have to take out a loan and pay any interest.

What a concept—pay less interest and keep more of your money!

6. **Build a New Income Stream** – What better way to use your extra income than to grow another income stream? The true purpose of money should be to make money. If you don't need it to survive, then why not use your extra income to your advantage to increase your monthly cash flow and become financially independent?

7. **Pay Down Debt** – Paying off your mortgage, vehicle, or credit cards is a great use for an extra income stream. If you can avoid paying tons of interest on a loan by making extra payments on existing debt, then you could be on your way to financial freedom.

8. **Diversified Income Sources** – Any good stockbroker will tell their customers the number one rule as an investor is to build a diversified portfolio to reduce risk. If you would diversify your investments, why wouldn't you do the same with your income streams? Creating multiple income streams allows a person to diversify the various cash flow sources that are coming in. In the event one dries up, there are other sources of income to lessen the loss.

9. **Build a Holiday Fund** – This is something my wife and I recently did after I earned some extra freelance income. Instead of stressing about how we will pay for all the extra holiday expenses this year, we simply designated this alternative income stream to be used for the holidays.

10. **Take Control of Income** – When was the last time you got a raise at work? Even if you have received one in the past year, there is no guarantee you will be getting one next year, especially the way the economy is behaving. Do yourself a favor and take control of your finances by creating multiple streams of income. That way you have the power to give yourself a raise anytime you like!

The purpose behind this book is to show you, the reader, that there are so many ways to make income in this world. We must be willing to open up our thinking and surround ourselves with individuals who are living the life of entrepreneurship. For many people in this world, jobs are not taking care of the bills and we are finding ourselves deeper and deeper in holes of debt, frustration, and confusion. We hope that you will learn from our authors, and if there is anyone that you identify with, we encourage you to contact them directly. We have made it so you can connect with all of our authors on social media and more.

In this book you will get a chance to get answers from our authors. The great thing about our authors is that they also are all different in personality and experience. We allowed them to answer the questions with as little or as much detail as they felt was needed. We asked them questions about how long it took for them to obtain success in their industries, what their daily life activities consist of and more! Enjoy your read, and congratulations on making multiple streams of income.

Taurea Vision Avant

Industry - Public Speaking
Instagram.com/VisionAvant
Facebook.com/VisionAvant
Periscope.tv/VisionAvant
Twitter.com/VisionAvant
Google.com/+TaureaAvantVision
LinkedIn.com/in/visionavant
www.TaureaAvant.com

Taurea Avant started her entrepreneurial career back in 1999 as a bail bondsman. She enjoyed being able to be in control of her time, but after a year in that industry, she learned that her fear of guns would probably keep her from being able to really excel in that field. Plus, most of her clients needed her at times of the year when, to be honest, she wasn't in town. She then went on to become a licensed life insurance agent. After taking her life and health test three times and finally passing, she quickly learned that she didn't have a passion for selling life insurance. In fact, her first presentation was her last presentation. She was given a lead, drove up to the home she was to present to, got scared, and just drove off. Then she went on to try different types of businesses from selling knives, vacuum cleaners, telecommunication services and more. In 2004, she was offered an opportunity to become a television host for a local late-night show. This is where Taurea got her first taste of learning how to effectively communicate. Like a lot of people that we may come into contact with today, Taurea had a fear of networking and communicating. Her fear was rooted in the ultimate fear of rejection. She had to learn to get over this fear if she desired to be able to the best TV host possible. While all this was going on in her life, she also graduated from Hampton University with a degree in computer science and then went on to work in "Corporate America" for 2 years of her life. She, like most college graduates today, struggled to land a job, going from temp job to temp job. In 2006, she was able to obtain a position as a database administrator with a salary of less than $30,000 per year.

It wasn't until 2007 that Taurea's life changed completely! October 2006, Taurea found out her father was diagnosed with stage IV lung cancer. This was probably one of the most traumatic experiences in her life. Her mother already passed to cirrhosis of the liver when she was 11 years old. Her father had become her everything and she dependent upon him in so many ways. She never believed that ultimately this disease would take his life. However, 7 months later her father was gone. A month after he passed, she moved to Atlanta to start a new life.

In 2008, Taurea started her own multimedia company called "Echelon Media" with a partner in Virginia. She was the web designer and he was the video editor. She invested more than $40,000 into this business and was certain it would be the beginning of an incredible and profitable future. Unfortunately, there was nothing profitable about it, although you could say it was incredible! At the end of the year, she had earned only $800.

It was not what Taurea expected one bit! However, one thing Taurea learned is that *"failing doesn't make you a failure, it's giving up that does."* In 2009, Taurea started working in a home-based business—also known as multilevel marketing or network marketing. In her first 6 months of being in the business, she earned more than six figures. In that company she was also introduced to a new concept that she never knew much about and that was personal development. She went to her first conference in 2009 where she spent a little under $500. She absolutely fell in love with personal growth and that's where her real journey to success started.

In 2010, Taurea decided she needed to partner with a company that stood on strong leadership, a system with integrity, and a product that she could promote. She joined another home business company (name not provided due to copyright laws) and was able to follow great principles that have now earned her more than $1,000,000 in earnings in the past five years. She is one of the top 5% income earners in her industry, and she has no plans of stopping anytime soon!

At the beginning of 2015, Taurea decided to launch the Show Your Success Workshop and her S.Y.S.T.E.M. mastery program. With the chances of many not understanding her passion or even disagreeing with her vision, she still made a decision to go all the way in. The reason she decided to start these events and programs is because she saw a never ending number of business owners who really didn't know what to do in building their businesses. She had many friends who were being taken advantage of and wasting a lot of money with no results. As small business owners, the last thing we want to do is waste money. She personally knew hundreds of leaders in the industry who weren't able to obtain success like hers, even though they worked their butts off. She wanted to be able to create a program and events that were tailored to changing that. Some of her goals are to be able to show business owners some of the following:

- How to brand and market yourself without spending a fortune.
- How to separate yourself from everyone else in your business.
- How to increase your profits without spending more than you are making.

The difference in Taurea and other people offering the same services is that she actually has had the success. There are a lot of people that teach on theory; she teaches on principle!

Taurea wanted to share her experiences in public speaking because it was her speaking skills that allowed her to run multimillion dollar home-based businesses as well as launch a million dollar workshop program that is currently on tour across the United States and in multiple countries in the world.

Taurea has been able to speak in many countries with more than 10,000 people in a setting. Her goal is to show entrepreneurs how to increase their speaking skills regardless of what kind of business they are in. It is your skill to deliver information that will make a difference in making hundreds to thousands to millions.

Her mission in life is to directly impact the lives of 10,000,000 men and women in mind, body, and soul one event at a time!

How long have you been in your industry?
I've been successfully speaking since 2009, but I really started in the world of speaking back in 2003 when I was offered an opportunity to host a local television show. It's kind of ironic because all of my life, I've really been more so of an introvert, but in certain environments I would turn into someone else. I call her my inner "Sasha Fierce." Hosting this show happened to be one of those examples.

Why did you get into your industry?

Honestly, I just fell into the world of speaking. For me, I've always known my voice was powerful. I used to sell items over the phone when I was 16 years old and learned the power behind a voice, but I honestly used to hate the feeling of convincing people. I'm still that way today. I don't like to feel like I have to convince people to buy, but I do love the feeling of empowering someone to take action. I got into a home-based business in 2009 and just was looking for a way to make some extra money. I decided to make speaking my business when I earned my first comma check (check over one thousand dollars) speaking to small groups. Initially I didn't really want to speak in front of people, but I learned quickly that if I wanted to sell these products or services, I would need to learn to speak better.

When it comes to being an entrepreneur, what do you love most about it?

I love the fact that I am in control of my own time. It's the one commodity that we can't ever get back, so my time is so valuable to me. Honestly, I love to be home watching a movie in the middle of a workday. I love to take last minute trips to places I want to visit. I love to be able to do what I want to do when I want to do it. I even love the fact that I can work when I want and where I want to. When you are not in control of your own time, you can't have the pleasure of doing things like this. There is nothing like freedom of time without being worried about money. Now there is an additional blessing of being an entrepreneur, and that is the blessing of empowering other entrepreneurs to take action. That's what's so incredible about speaking. You have a chance to change someone's life through words, and that feeling of appreciation never gets old.

What would you consider the pros about being in your industry?

The pros are that you have the opportunity to make a lot of money as a speaker. I know speakers that make several six figures in a month just from speaking on a stage. Another pro about being a speaker is that your network becomes massive. There has not been one time I have ever spoken and not met a new influencer. I'm always looking to expand my network with go-getters, and when you speak in front of people, you receive immediate respect from the audience. You just never know who may be watching you. This has been a huge blessing for my business. One speaking gig can lead to many gigs for the year.

Were you required to make any financial and/or time investments to get started?

Not including when I hosted the TV show, but in 2009, when I began to credit myself as successful speaker, my initial investment started at $300. I enrolled into a home-based business and was traveling the country speaking about this product. Now while some may not see being in a home-based business as a public speaking gig, I totally would. The truth about the industry is that if you are not able to paint a clear picture and have the audience believe they can succeed, then they will not buy the opportunity. So for me this absolutely was public speaking. It wasn't about sales because in today's world people don't like to be sold to. People like to buy. They just need someone that can paint the picture clear enough for them to believe they can do the work. That is what I did. I have since then been to workshops and conferences to help with building better relationships and bettering my craft. In 2014, I decided to start my own company doing workshops and speaking across the country. The initial investment to get that started was less than $2000, which was really just for marketing. My business cards, business license, website, social media, and CRM programs all ran me less than $2000 to get started. I've also spent as much as $6000 for one 4-day workshop. Now to get started, you don't have to invest as much as I have, but you have to start somewhere to get started.

What are the statistics of success in your industry?

1. 3 out of 4 people or 75% of individuals suffer from a fear of speaking in public. I happen to be one of those people who fought through the fear. It is incredible to note that the fear of public speaking tops the greatest fears that trouble people according to a popular survey. In fact, this fear tops the fear of death, spiders, heights, and confined spaces. This shows that people feel public speaking is a greater torture than

10

any of these—including death itself. Surely public speaking cannot be that difficult if you try.

2. Men and women are equally affected by the fear of public speaking. However, more men than women seek assistance with speaking anxiety.

3. There are different kinds of speakers. I would like to provide you with these types to give you better clarity. While these are not necessarily statistics, I think they are great pieces of information for anyone who is interested in getting into this field of public speaking.

   o **Persuasive Public Speaking** – The art of persuasion has developed into a unique field of public speaking. Traditional persuasion uses a set of techniques that when employed skillfully will allow the speaker to move the audience to adopt a new thought, idea, concept, or way of doing things.

   o **Informative Public Speaking** –The goal is to inform the audience about the topic of the presentation. It requires a context that will allow the audience to take in the information and make it usable.

   o **Demonstrative Public Speaking** – Like informative speaking, demonstrative speaking attempts to demonstrate how to do something. It is easier to remember how to do something when we actually see it being done. An example could be that of a knife salesman. I actually attempted to sell knives one time but never got to the point of the speaking. I was terrified, and at that time allowed my fear to handicap me.

   o **Motivational Public Speaking** – A motivational public speaker uses stories, anecdotes, illustrations, and allegories to engage the audience and share with the audience a lesson or moral that will uplift, inspire, and/or have an impact on those who listen. One of my favorite motivational speakers would be Les Brown. He absolutely is an incredible storyteller and can motivate anyone in my opinion.

- **Debate** – Debate is the verbal sparring and comes in several forms. When I think of debaters, I think of politicians.
- **Workshop or Seminar Speaking** – This is where you may have a combination of motivational and informational speaking, but informational speaking is more common. This is what I would categorize myself as. I often title myself as an educator. When people go to workshops, they are typically coming to learn a specific skill set.

What is the average income in your industry?
The average annual salary for a speaker was $88,000 as of 2013, according to the job site Indeed. Many are self-employed and pay themselves salaries from their profits. Making this kind of income as a speaker requires a lot of back end work. Earn more than $50,000 a year as a speaker requires that you know how to find the events to speak at. Until you get to a point where people are seeking you out daily, you must be willing to roll up your sleeves and find these opportunities. Also, I would like to add that not every speaking opportunity means you get paid up front. The product or service you are there to promote is where the real money would come into play.

When it comes to success in your industry, what are 3 main tips you would give to those interested in doing what you do.
- Know what kind of speaker you want to be and what it is that you are selling.
- Study, study, study! Do not be afraid to invest in strengthening your skills. I see too many people who believe they are capable, knowledgeable speakers. There is a big difference between having knowledge of the product or service or topic you are speaking on versus. actually knowing how to deliver it to your audience.
- Be willing to reach out to many more people than you expect to respond back. For me to get in front of people, I would have to reach out to at least ten organizers before I get on eyes. If you don't have people blowing up

your phone or email, then you have to reach out to organizers and let them know you are out there.

When actively working in your industry, what does a day (or week) look like for you?
Wow! Well, a day in the life of Taurea Avant is never the same as another day. What I will say is my daily goal is to lock in more opportunities to get in front of more people to speak. When I wake up, I start off with listening to my daily bible app. Then I work out and speak my affirmations. I then read my definite major purpose aloud before getting dressed. You most definitely should connect with me so I can show you more about identifying your definite major purpose. I typically work from home every day so my commute is about one minute downstairs to my office. Then, I check my calendar to see what tasks I set for the day before. On a weekly basis, my goal is to be able to reach out to at least 20 to 30 organizers for upcoming events that could be an opportunity for me to speak or host an event. Once per week I set up automation for my social media accounts so during the week, I can take time to communicate with others. I have a few other businesses as well, so I will handle things with some of those companies. All in all, my days stay busy, but of course I also do my best to bring balance and rest to my life. My goals for my speaking business are to host two seven-hour workshops per month, two mini-workshops per month, four to five conference calls with other entrepreneurs per month, and daily quick power calls for my social media followers.

Do you have a mentor?
I absolutely have a mentor. For me there have been mentors during different phases of my business. I have a spiritual mentor who I can call to talk about everything in life and get fed spiritually, but I also have a business mentor who knows more than just about my business. He literally knows everything about me. This is important because he has to know why I may do things a certain way if he is going to mentor me. I will say that a lot of people are not actually ready to be mentored. I've found that many people just want cheerleaders rather than mentors or coaches. There have been times when I did not agree with my mentors, but if I were to agree with them, I would be where they

13

are in life. Since I'm not, I choose to have them as mentors. Because they see that I'm following the instructions, they choose to continue mentoring me. Having a mentor has played a major role in my life because I tried to get to success for so long and had no idea why my actions were not working. The truth behind success is just doing things isn't enough to get you to success, but doing things a certain way that gets you to success. That is why mentorship is valuable. Some of the things I've learned from my mentors include

- Steps to setting goals,
- What to do with a dollar, and
- How to get your audience to engage

Has being in your industry helped you to expand to other industries?

Speaking has led to so many business opportunities for me. I got several requests for a book, so I decided to write one, which helped in expanding my speaking career as well. I've been able to launch my vision clothing and gear line, as well as many other ventures including my online educational program. This is all because of the following I have created through different speaking opportunities. Many of these opportunities are inbound (Periscope, conference calls, workshops, etc.) and outbound, where I've been hired to speak.

If someone was to come to you for help, what would be the first thing you would tell them in regards to getting started in your industry.

Know what you want to speak about. I've seen some people who want to speak on every topic you can think of. The challenge with that is you will confuse the prospect. Single it down to about 4 topics. Also make sure you have a coach to guide you in your journey.

Outside of working (in your industry) what is your favorite thing to do?

I love watching movies. My favorite movies are motivational movies. Some of my all-time favorites are *Peaceful Warrior*, *Little Boy*, *War Room*, *Joy*, and *Independence Day*. There are plenty more, but I'm sure if you haven't seen any of these, you will get absolutely motivated. I mostly enjoy going to the movies in the middle of the day so I can have majority of the theater to myself. It's just one of the blessings of being an entrepreneur.

Do you provide coaching or resources to anyone who wants to further educate themselves in your industry?
Yes, I do offer an online educational program where my main goal is to show you how to deliver a speech that sells. In the program you learn how to design your speech and sell your product or service. The key is to always have people wanting to stay connected to you whenever you speak. That is part of what you learn with my program.

Is there anything you don't necessarily love about the industry?
I would say that I don't like the selfishness of some "speakers" that I meet. Sorry, one thing you will learn about me is I will always be truthful and express my feelings as long as it doesn't directly hurt someone. I put quotations around speakers because I believe that when you truly understand your purpose and your purpose is to be a speaker, then you wouldn't be as selfish. I teach a lot of my students to reach out to organizers and offer to help without expecting anything in return. It can make you look butter, but the law of sowing and reaping is true for everyone. The more that you serve, the more you will increase your chances to serve. In fact, because I am so serious about this, I am now doing a conference call every Monday where I invite other entrepreneurs to be a part of this call and be interviewed. However, to be interviewed on the call, you actually have to listen in. I'm doing this to show others that if we learn to support more, we can have more. I truly believe that there is no need to complain about something if you aren't willing to find a way to better that situation.

What favorite marketing strategies have you used to help with building your business?
Social media is one of my favorite marketing techniques. I've fallen in love with using live broadcasting and conference calls in alignment with social media.

My books have been an amazing marketing technique for me as well. It's what I like to call a premium business card. Everyone loves to hire authors to speak to their group.

I've also used the strategy of collaboration opportunities from calls to free workshops. These have helped me tremendously. Working together with other people will always increase your network with more people.

What are 3 books that you recommend for success in your industry?

- *Show Your Success to Effective Marketing Mastery* – Taurea Vision Avant
- *Platform: Get Noticed in a Noisy World* – Michael Hyatt
- *Public Speaking for Success* – Arthur R. Pell & Dale Carnegie

If there was one thing you may have done differently in your industry when you got started, what would it have been?
Me personally, I would not change my journey. I am in love with my life journey. If I could have done anything differently, it would have been hiring a coach much earlier instead of trying to do everything myself. I have ended up spending thousands of dollars and countless hours doing it myself. It wasn't until I had direct coaching from someone who had direct success as a speaker that I was able to get better immediate results. I'm not saying you can't succeed if you don't get a coach, but it's always easier to have someone in your life who has had the success. Yes, there are great books and podcasts but the issue is that books and podcasts can't really give you feedback.

What is your favorite quote?
"Vision is the art of seeing what's invisible to others. So don't allow those who don't see what you see to break your focus. Don't look left. Don't look right. Stay focused forward on what God has for you and all will be well!" – Taurea Vision Avant

Special thanks to the following

CHARMAINE SMITH
MARY KAY INDEPENDENT CONSULTANT
FACEBOOK.COM/CHARMAINESMITHMARYKAYINDEPENDENTBEAUTYC
ONSULTANT

CHERILL R. ASHTON, B.S., M.S.
CONSULTANT, HOSTESS, MOTIVATIONAL SPEAKER, PERFORMING ARTS
PROFESSIONAL, WRITER
FACEBOOK.COM/BLONDEACTRESSASHTON

DEBI BELLVILLE
BREAKTHROUGH TRANSFORMATION SPECIALIST
FACEBOOK.COM/DEBISTRANSFORMISSION

DOROTHY TRAVIS

ELISSA MITCHELL
MARY KAY INDEPENDENT
CONSULTANTFACEBOOK.COM/ELISSA.MITCHELL.73

FELIX GRIFFIN
BIZ SAVY ENTREPRENEUR
FACEBOOK.COM/FELIXGRIFFIN

JAMES & NATASHA ROACH
AUTHORS, ENTREPRENEURIAL COUPLE & PUBLIC SPEAKER
FACEBOOK.COM/MRMRSROACH
WWW.MRANDMRSROACH.COM

KRISTIN L. MORRIS
ORGANIC HAIRCOLORIST/STYLIST/MUA/NYR ORGANIC BEAUTY
EXPERT
FACEBOOK.COM/KRISTINLAYNESTYLE
FACEBOOK.COM/GLAMORGANICDIVA

LAKEISHA PARNELL
CONFIDENCE COACH, SPEAKER, ADVOCATE, AUTHOR

FACEBOOK.COM/LAKEISHA.PARNELL
WWW.LAKEISHAPARNELL.COM

DR. LaSHONDA JACKSON-DEAN, PhD/DM JDI
PROFESSIONAL SOLUTIONS AUTHOR AND PROFESSOR
FACEBOOK.COM/DR.LaSHONDAJACKSONDEANDMCORNELIUS
PATTERSON

MARION SHEPHERD
HOME BASED BUSINESS
FACEBOOK.COM/MARIONSHEP

MATTHEW GOLD
HOME BUSINESS
ENTREPRENEURFACEBOOK.COM/MATTHEWVINCENTGOLD

QUIANA DIXON

SHARON PORTER
HEALTH & WELLNESS
TOTALLIFECHANGES.COM/SHARONHPORTER

SUSAN "COACH SUSIE" STANLEY
HOLISTIC SUCCESS COACH
FACEBOOK.COM/HEALTHCOACH.SUZ

Lee Chapman

Industry - Precious Metals
Instagram.com/LeeChapman1969
Facebook.com/lee.chapman.1460
Twitter.com/LeeRossChapman
Google.com/+/LeeChapman
Linkedin.com/in/lee-chapman-92ab6875
www.AdelaideGoldBuyers.com.au
www.MrLeeChapman.com

Lee Chapman was born in 1969 in Adelaide, South Australia, and was raised on a small, 2,000-acre farm 75 miles from the capital city. His family's farm did not produce a lot of money. While he was bought up in a loving family, they did not have the luxuries most families had. Lee didn't realize this until he went to school and found out that other kids didn't shop at second hand opportunity shops.

Lee's father had a heart attack, and while it didn't kill him, they sold the farm. When he finished school, he applied for the air force as a pilot, but was turned down on medical grounds. Lee soon found work in the local supermarket and fast food hamburger outlet. He did this for about a year.

Lee applied for a job in a mass production jewelry factory as a jewelry finisher. He worked in this factory for approximately eight years learning all facets of jewelry production. While it paid the bills, he hated being told what to do, when he could have lunch, etc.

Lee had a moment one day. He had a very bad two weeks during which his grandfather had passed, he'd caught his girlfriend cheating on him, and he was working a job that he hated. He had two maxed out Visa cards and $5 in his pocket, and he needed fuel in the car.

Lee pulled in the gas station and as he went through the ash tray looking for coins to pay for gas, his dream car pulled into the lot. Lee cursed the creator. It just wasn't fair. He went into the station and paid with $5 worth of coins covered in apple scented car deodorant dust. He could feel people judging his poverty.

As Lee walked from the station, he was done and wanted the ground to swallow him whole. As he passed the dream V8 coupe, the owner pulled his wheelchair across his lap.

It hit Lee like a ton of bricks. He did not know how that man became disabled or how he got that car. He did know that where he was in life was a total sum of all the decisions he had made.

Lee said yes to the factory job, to seeing that girl, and to getting the Visa cards.

Lee knew he could change, and all he had to do was copy successful people. He found out successful people are self-employed. He copied successful jewelers and started a jewelry repair business. It was scary, but it produced an income and gave Lee a real taste of freedom even though he worked as a sub-contractor for a major jewelry chain store.

Lee soon went out on his own and independently opened his own gold buying and bullion selling business, SA Gold Traders. He and his wife worked on their business, copying and studying other gold buyers and bullion dealers. They applied for a Perth Mint distributorship and passed all the checks.

In their second full year of business they turned over $3.2 million in business and are currently the largest Perth Mint Distributors in South Australia by volume.

Lee and his wife have used technology to teach business principles across to many men and women across the country who want more from life.

They continue to grow by helping and touching as many people as possible, and all this happened because they stepped out in faith that the world would give to them if they just gave in to themselves first.

How long have you been in the industry?
I have been involved in the precious metals industry since 1988. Basically, straight out of high school I worked in a supermarket in the fruit and vegetable section, and during the summer I worked in a local fish and hamburger shop. I landed a job in the jewelry industry working in a mass production jewelry factory at the age of 19 in 1988.

When it comes to being an entrepreneur what do you love most about it?
For me, I got to a stage where I got sick and tired of being under the control of a manager and a boss. I made a decision to be my

21

own boss. The biggest payoff is being in control of what I do—when I can spend time with family and the flexibility it brings. But really what I love is being significant in the lives of others by helping people become more and to believe in themselves and watching people succeed in their purpose. I really like helping people get what they want, be that financially, spiritually, or just some life guidance. I just love the freedom it brings for me to follow my passions in life.

What are the pros of your industry?
As far as jewelry is concerned, the pros are that it's an industry that has been around since the dawn of time regardless of the economy. There has always been a need for jewelers and the products they sell, as well as the repair of these products. That's without mentioning the investment in precious metals and the trading of gold and silver. It is truly the money of kings.

The best opportunity at the moment worldwide is in the scrap gold and silver market. The demand for gold and silver has never been higher, and the cost to mine it has increased to a point of not being financially feasible for mining companies. The recycled gold market is increasing, and the term has now been coined as urban gold mining. The amount of gold and silver held in private hands in the form of coins and jewelry with in the USA alone would be in the 100s if not 1000s of tons. There is still room for anyone to start today.

Were you required to make any financial or time investments to get started?
My story is long, but I basically worked my way through my industry in the jewelry factory learning all sections of the industry including hand making, stone setting, and gold refining. In my own time, I did a jewelry beginner's course at a local community school. It soon became apparent that I had most of the skills being taught, and students started asking me questions. I decided that I had to go out on my own, yet I didn't believe in myself. The qualified jeweler who taught me went out and started his own business so I went and worked for him. This lasted a year, and then I went out on my own. I was scared and frightened as I had never owned a business before. The

opportunity came up to be the onsite jeweler at a local Westfield shopping center. I was scared as I thought, "What could possible go wrong?" At the worst, I could go back to getting a job. The initial investment cost about $2000 in tools. I did this for a number of years, but because I was a subcontractor to the jewelry chain store, I was limited to how much I could charge. As the price of gold increased, my profit margin decreased to such a point I was only $50 better off from working a job. I closed that business and got another job. Using my military experience, I got a job as a security guard in the main shopping precinct in Adelaide. In my spare time, I looked at other ways to make money. There was a very large jewelry buying business that bought secondhand jewelry and resold it at near retail. I decided that to be successful all you had to do was trace success.

"Buying scrap gold and silver is where it's at." With $100, I started buying scrap gold and silver jewelry from friends and family and reselling it to the big jewelry business. From that $100, it wasn't long before I had increased it to $2000. This really helped with paying extra bills and paying for the kids' school fees.

I started doing jewelry gold buying parties where I would see five to eight ladies at once and buy their unwanted jewelry. I then paid the host a portion of the profit, and from this I booked other parties. It was a win/win as the host made money, the guests made money, and so did I. At this stage, happy wife happy life kicked in.

All this was done with no overheads run after hours from peoples' homes. In most cases, the jewelry party went for two hours, and often I would make between $600 to $1000 gross profits. That's an average of $500 per hour without a degree making the same money a lawyer charges per hour.

To summarize, I started scrap jewelry buying with $100. However, when I started my full time scrap gold buying business with an office in the city, I remortgaged the family home and started with $45,000. That turned into $3.2 million in turnover in its second year.

What are the statistics of success in your industry?
My industry is broad and exact stats are hard to gather. I can tell you from experience that about 1 percent of the people who start in making jewelry who try to sell it or those who try to break into the manufacturing jewelry, reach the point of owning a store. The industry is changing rapidly. I would not recommend going down this track simply because the average girl doesn't care about real gold and silver as long as it matches her outfit. This is why costume jewelry is so big.

I believe there is an opportunity to import costume jewelry from China or India and resell it. I have seen an increase in people buying from aliexpress.com and reselling on Ebay®.

I can tell you that other scrap gold buyers have done very well because of worldwide inflation. The cost of goods has increased faster than the average household income. People have been forced to sell their unwanted jewelry. I don't see this trend going down any time soon. Also the cost of mining has increased, causing the recycled gold market to increase. It really is a golden opportunity.

What is the average income in your industry?
From knowing other scrap gold buyers and bullion dealers in my area I can say the average income is around $80,000 to $100,000 per year.

They actually have businesses that turn over much more than this. The above figures are what may be stated on their tax returns. Being a full time business owner has certain tax benefits, allowing the business to buy a car and pay for uniforms etc. You can pick up more income and keep more money by topping up your 401(k).

It's wise to get a good accountant or seek some advice about the laws in your state before you start. A good accountant should give you some free time. I suggest you ask someone that is successful for their advice on an accountant. My advice is when you call say that you are calling to arrange an appointment to interview an accountant to see if he/she suits your business.

This makes the accountant work harder to win your contract and takes the nerves from you and places them onto the accountant.

When it comes to success in your industry, what are the 3 main tips to those interested in doing what you do?
Oh, that's tough. I would have to say before doing anything ask yourself one question, and that is, "Why?" Why do you want money? To be honest, it's not the money, but what you can do with it. Visualize that thing in your mind. Because there are many ways to make money—both legal and illegal—it's the why that will keep you focused when things get tough.

- Learn as much as you can about gold and silver jewelry.
- Study how people make money with jewelry buying and jewelry loans during the depression, because times like these will come again in the near future.
- Start today in some small way. Get some money together and just make the decision that from this day on you will not be the same person and will continue to grow into the person who achieves the dreams in your mind.

When actively working in your industry what does a day or week look like?
I can tell you that it's taken some time to get where I am today. My day starts when I wake at about 7 am. I don't have an alarm. I often take the kids to school. I get to the office and open between 9:30 a.m. and 10 a.m. I often have appointments from clients who have called earlier in the week.

I have a mixture of scrap gold clients, gold and silver investment clients, and customers wanting loans using jewelry as collateral. Typically, I buy between $5,000 and $10,000 in scrap a week, making approximately 18 to 20 percent on my money. I also have clients buying gold and silver bullion for investment. Clients buying bullion from $10,000 upwards two or three times a week is not uncommon.

Do you have mentor? What have you learned from them?
Yes, I have a mentor and business coach. The reason is it's great to have someone to follow and guide you. There are many pitfalls in business, and you can't make all the mistakes yourself. It's wise to listen to others with more experience. A mentor and coach will guide you and give unbiased advice and keep you accountable. Most importantly he or she will build you up, cheer for you, and keep you going and believe in you when the days don't seem as bright.

Has being in your industry helped to expand into other industries?
Being in the precious metal/bullion/jewelry industry has not directly helped, but being in business for myself definitely has. You see, when you make the decision to be the captain of your destiny, things seem clearer. You walk differently and talk differently. And while it's true, "it's not what you know but who you know," I also believe the missing part to this saying is "become the person people want to know."

I would not be in this book helping people I most likely will never meet if I hadn't just believed in myself just a little and taken a chance on my own ability. What is life without some risk and adventure? The scariest thing is just starting. I found out later that I should have believed in myself a lot sooner.

If someone was to come to you for help what would be the first thing you would tell them in regard to getting started in your industry?
Before going any further, have a clear idea why you want to make money. As I said before, it's not usually the money, it's what can be done with it. You will need a clear idea in mind. Once this is achieved, your mind will open to opportunities everywhere.

With making money in scrap gold buying, I would recommend gaining as much information on the jewelry industry in your area or culture as possible.

What are the common items encountered in your area or country? For example, coins, jewelry, silverware, etc.

Look at how big you want to go. Do you want to make a few hundred dollars extra per month to just tie over the monthly budget, or do you really want to make serious income? And if it's the second option, how much? You need a definite number that you want to make in a year.

My mentor told me fuzzy goals get fuzzy results; clear goals get clear results.

Seek out information courses on jewelry or gold buying. I recommend buying the book, *Guide to Investing in Gold and Silver: Protect your Financial Future* by Michael Maloney.

If you have never had a business before, I recommend—and I honestly believe—you join some sort of multilevel marketing business because it will teach you about belief in yourself, products, goal setting, dream building and people skills. It's also cheap to start and you will be following a proven system. Furthermore, it gives you access to successful people to follow and use as mentors.

This will teach you a lot in a very short time, and it's cheap. I have been involved in two MLM businesses, and to be honest it has paid off more than any college business program ever could—without the student debt.

Outside of working in your industry, what is your favorite thing to do?

Besides spending time with my young family, I have discovered my real purpose and that is to help men and young males in western society realize the strength and importance they still play in this world. I feel political correctness has smashed the male ego too much, and I love helping guide young men into adulthood and revealing to men they have what it takes to be a part of something larger than themselves.

Is there anything you don't like about your industry?
Sure there is. I can say because of the changing gold price, your profit is never constant, but when you buy on the right side at the right time, you can make huge profits. Also, sometimes the competition will copy you or come into your area, but that's business. If you are afraid of competition, you shouldn't be in business, but I realized I am an original so I can't be copied anyway.

If you are not schooled in the finer details of jewelry buying, you can often buy a fake and a small mistake can be costly.

Earning trust from the community can take a while because some have done the wrong thing in the past. My advice is to always be fair and honest, and word will get around that you are a fair trader.

What has been some of your favorite marketing strategies?
I am a big fan of guerilla marketing because it's cheap. I went to the bank and got a hand full of plastic coin bags. I got $20 worth of 5-cent pieces and placed the coin and a business card saying "Need extra money? We buy gold" in each one with my details.

I dropped these at bus stops, car parking lots, busy street shopping malls, changing room in department stores, even near banks and AT's. When people see a money bag with a coin in it, their curiosity is piqued as there might be more money inside. It worked great.

I also looked at an industry with similar clients to mine—typically women thirty to sixty years old. I went to a local beautician and asked if they had any vouchers or sample packs I could give out to promote their business. I found hand cream was a winner. In return, they had to hand out my cards to their best clients.

This worked great as women came into my business, and I bought a couple hundred dollars' worth of jewelry from them. I would give them a free hand cream sample and beauty voucher.

This made them feel special as ladies love free stuff. When they caught up with their friends, what do you think they talked about? You guessed it—my business. Word of mouth referrals are awesome, and it didn't cost me a cent.

It's called cross-business promotion. This works well with someone willing to do the same for you. Remember, use businesses that are in line to your client base but not in direct opposition to you.

Do you provide coaching or resources to anyone who wants to educate themselves in your industry?
Yes, I have a series of educational videos on the scrap gold and silver buying and bullion trading in physical metal.

I describe all the tools and calculations needed to work out buy and sell prices.

The videos are full of useful tips and tricks that I have gained since 1988. I designed this series to save new gold buyers time and stress while making maximum profit by reading how world events dictate the movement of precious metals and how to place you on the right side of most buying opportunities.

My videos can be found on my websites

- www.adelaidegoldbuyers.com.au
- www.makemoneyaustralia.com.au

When contacting me, use the promo code (BOOK#1 USA) to receive additional free training videos valued at $300 and discounts on future training material.

If there was one thing you may have done differently in your industry when you got started, what would it have been?
I have learned a lot of lessons, and to be honest there wasn't any one to learn from, so I have made literally every mistake.

If I had to pick one thing to do differently, it would be to have started out on my own a lot sooner. If I had my time over again,

I would jump right in with no hesitation and start working for myself straight from high school.

What's your favorite quote?
"One person can make a difference and everyone should try."— *John F. Kennedy*

Special thanks to the following:

Mr. Ben Birkett
Jeweller, Watchmaker
Birkett Watches
Facebook.com/Birkett-Watches-Australia

Mr. Ian Lumsden
Business owner Sales performance improvement
Prosell
Facebook.com/ianmlmcoach

Lee Chapman
Business owner, Author, Speaker, Life Teacher
SA Gold Traders
Facebook.com/SA-Gold-Traders

Mr. Adam Neukother
Business owner, Network Marketing
Facebook.com/adam.neukother

Mr. Robert Adams
Business owner, Network Marketing
Facebook.com/ROBADAMS5

Belinda Chapman
Business owner, Life Teacher
SA Gold Traders
Facebook.com/belinda.chapman.39

Alison Fong
Business owner, Network Marketing
Facebook.com/alison.fong.18

Mr. Jason T.M. Chapman
Business owner, Entrepreneur

Karissa Zappelli
Business owner and manager
Forrest House Accomodation
Facebook.com/Forrest-House

Cissy Agurs

Industry – Cleaning Services
Instagram.com/IamCissya
Facebook.com/IamCissy
Persicope.tv/IamCissya
Twitter.com/IamCissya
Google.com/+/Iamcissy
Linkedin.com/in/Iamcissy
www.IamCissy.com

Cissy Agurs is the proud mother of three children: Alexander, Taylar, and Leslie, who inspired her to create a business that would leave a lasting legacy. She started ATL&C Cleans, LLC, in 2005. The moniker ATL represents the names of each of her children, and this serves as a constant reminder and source of motivation in all that she does. Cissy has successfully navigated ATL&C into a 70+client/customer portfolio with 32 amazing employees with service locations in two states. Cissy's greatest lessons is to never compromise your mission and values for money, and allow disrespect to pay you.

How long have you been in your industry?

I have been running ATL&C Cleans for more than ten years. However, I have been a part of the cleaning industry for much longer than that. My mother worked for a furniture company, and the owner would let my brothers and I come in to work on Saturday to dust and vacuum and make extra money. During that time, I realized how focused and relaxed I felt while cleaning and how it felt to serve in that way. So Dionne Watkins, my sister-in-law, and I started cleaning houses in the neighborhood. These discoveries revealed my passion for cleaning, and this knowledge helped lead me into my business. Inspired by my desire to leave a legacy to my children, I started ATL&C Cleans in 2005. Naming the company after my children Alexander, Taylar and Leslie serves as a constant reminder that my children are my greatest motivator. I operate my business based on Christian principles. I have more than twenty years of cleaning experience, with more than seventy-two satisfied clients and thirty-five employees. We offer commercial, residential, and custom cleaning services. We provide a complete selection of janitorial service programs tailored to each of our client's requirements. We know that the janitorial services business is very competitive, so we work hard to offer you the highest level of service at the best possible price. It is this combination of price and value that has helped me build a great reputation locally.

Why did you get into your industry?

Cleaning has always been like a form of therapy for me, and it has made a significant impact on my life. When I realized how much I enjoyed serving through the avenue of cleaning, I decided to incorporate my passion and enthusiasm into a cleaning business. My business is a great opportunity for me to serve myself and to serve others.

When it comes to being an entrepreneur, what do you love most about it?

I love the freedom that it allows me with my time and my resources because that freedom gives me a greater opportunity to serve God and His people. I fulfill so many different roles (as an entrepreneur, as a mother, as a daughter, as a Christian—just to name a few) that I cannot allow someone else to be in charge of how I use my time and resources. The joy and privilege of being a mother has always come first, and I have always made my children a priority with all of my resources. Being an entrepreneur keeps me at the helm of responsibility and stewardship that I need to display at all times. That would not be possible if I was tied to someone else's vision for their company and not my own.

What would you consider the pros about being in your industry?

Being a woman in a male-dominated industry has allowed me to set a great example for others. I have learned what it means to make a place for my company in areas where there are many people who look like me but aren't in ownership roles. Fulfilling that role has allowed me the chance to support and encourage others who may be on similar journeys. It has also given me the chance to show other women, and minority women primarily, that they can achieve good success. Also, watching opportunities for minority business owners expand in this industry has been great. There was a time when opportunities for procuring contracts and growing your revenue in this industry were limited, and there was not much support to be found. It has been so exciting watching the connections grow, whether that has been through legislation and government regulations or through extended networking opportunities.

Were you required to make any financial and/or time investments to get started?
I started with a vacuum, a mop bucket and a $2000 investment. The time investment was considerable in the beginning also. I started with fourteen-hour days, six days a week, and I was working around sixty to eighty hours a week. I relied on my family very heavily during these times and had to make sure that everyone was part of creating a better model of success and financial independence for our family. Sometimes I would have to bring my children along with me to clean my locations. As the needs of my clients and customers grew and changed, I was able to make the necessary adjustments to meet their needs. I now work eighteen-hour days sometimes, but only six days a month.

What are the statistics of success in your industry?
According to sbdcnet.org, the cleaning services industry is currently a $46 billion industry.

According to bls.Gov, there are currently more than 929,540 employees in my industry. The median income is $9.67 per hour with an annual wage of $20,120.

What is the average income in your industry?
The average income is about $25,000, but there are opportunities to make much more as day to day porters or in some of the other industry avenues.

When it comes to success in your industry, what are 3 main tips you would give to those interested in doing what you do
- Always start in residential. You can take advantage of the chance to learn and get one-on-one feedback about the industry while you are growing. It also helps to ensure that you don't take on too much too fast. Don't let a dollar get you disrespected; don't let money dictate you.
- Make sure to never compromise your mission and values for money, and allow disrespect to pay you. This means never put up with anyone who doesn't respect you and your service. Every dollar is a needed dollar.

36

- Do everything with serving God in mind first. When you put your focus on serving God and His people, you can do so much more with what you have.

When actively working in your industry, what does a day (week) look like for you?

In the beginning, it was fourteen-hour days, six days per week. That's now down to twelve-hour days, six days a month. A normal day starts off with me redeeming time in prayer and meditation so that I can be equipped for the day. My most important job continues next as I take my children to school. This has always been a very special part of my day as I realize a lot of parents do not have the opportunity to spend this time with their children. I didn't for ten years because I worked for someone else. I take advantage of this time to continue to pour into them and build them into kingdom citizens. The next part of my day involves completing in-office tasks: responding to emails, returning calls, scheduling appointments, and working on contacts and my networks. Once I pick my children up from school, I take more time to connect with them. There have been lots of sacrifices I've had to make when it comes to my children, but I've always put them first and I have always allowed them to share their opinions about our lives. I will ask them if Mommy's working too much and if I need to change jobs. Of course they always say no, because they like the things that business ownership has provided for us.

I then head out into the field to work. There are times when I may need to inspect or clean locations, provide delivery of supplies, do interviews with potential candidates, or meet with client executives regarding services. My return home time is governed by how extensive my tasks are at that point and how quickly I need to move to make things happen. Some days I may have to clean *six* buildings by myself due to callouts or other reasons. My return home time can range from 11 p.m. to as late as 2 a.m. And then I start again the next day!

Do you have a mentor?

I currently have a business mentor, but I have not had a mentor in the cleaning industry. However, my brother, Tony Watkins, has been my rock; he has taught me a lot through his words and actions in business—he's my Hero. There are a few things I have learned that I would pass on to others.

- **Never mix business with personal matters**–Keep your business goals in front of you, and do not short change your vision. There is a space for everything and mixing business with personal is the first way to begin disruption in your operations.
- **Follow your instincts**–Always follow your first instinct; don't doubt yourself. God has given you the ability to serve in the ways that you do. Trust that.
- **Show up on time**–Being prompt lets your clients and customers know that you value your time, and theirs.
- **Always represent yourself well**–Putting your best foot forward and being presentable, polished, and timely goes a long way into building credibility and trust in your brand.
- **Operate in excellence**–Never leave a job incomplete, and always go above the expectations of your clients and customers.
- **Serve your purpose**–Remember that you didn't start a business to save the world; use your platform to serve your purpose.

Has being in your industry helped you to expand to other industries?
Yes! I am constantly challenging myself to ELEVATE my thinking to change my world. No fear or doubt lives within me! Hence, I continue to brainstorm new ideas. I started I Am Cissy, my personal brand of service in 2014. Under my brand, I have started a women's group called Cissy's Sister Circle. My vision is to ENCOURAGE women to live out their dreams and to never forget about you! Cissy's Sister Circle strives to positively impact like-minded women through community involvement, networking events, forums, and workshops that aspire to elevate their mindsets. It is also where I interact with members and share experiences of wisdom and support, elevating,

empowering, and encouraging individuals to live out their dreams. I also have a teenage mentoring group called Cissy's 3D Youth Ambassadors, consisting of teens between the ages of thirteen and eighteen. With this group, I help empower teens and youth to get ready for college and the world by serving the community in different events. I perform business consulting which helps to provide support to other entrepreneurs who are growing their own brands of business. I'm also a certified life coach for people on their journey to success, and I am launching a jewelry line in 2017. All of these ventures can be credited to the direct impact of ATL&C Cleans.

If someone was to come to you for help what would be the first thing you would tell them in regards to getting started in your industry?

I would tell them to know their why. Why are you doing what you do? And why is it important? A person's why is the one thing that will keep them motivated and help to encourage them when times are challenging. A person's why is what will determine how successful they can become. You must make sure that your why is strong enough to keep you going—through everything. My children are my why. I have always wanted to be there for them and to provide for them in excellent ways—my love for them and my commitment to them have kept me going.

Outside of working (in your industry) what is your favorite thing to do?

Spending quality time with my family and traveling. Both of these things provide me with a sense of fulfillment and help me to maintain my focus as I grow my businesses. They are avenues to increasing my ability to serve. I love being able to serve others in any ways that I can. I have a lot to give, and I take personal responsibility for serving as many people as I can along my path. God has blessed me to be in a position where I can offer service to others on a regular basis, and it blesses me to be able to do so no matter if I am with my family or traveling to be with family and friends.

Do you provide coaching or resources to anyone who wants to further educate themselves in your industry?
Yes. I provide coaching and resources to anyone who may seek out or show a need for my service. They will learn how to operate successfully in business, how to clean, how to deal with all types of people, and how to make great decisions. All of these learning paths present knowledge that is essential to the success of an entrepreneur.

Is there anything you don't necessarily love about the industry?
Well for me, there is not a specific thing that I don't like about the industry. What I would say is because you're dealing with so many different people, you have to leave your emotions at the door. For example, I have a contract with a large company that has over 200 people in it, so I'm dealing with 200 different personalities, and sometimes they want things done that are not in the contract. So I would say communication from the top down would help. If management or ownership would communicate clearly about ATL&C's duties, then it would lessen some of the issues that we face due to a simple lack of information from the staff.

What favorite marketing strategies have you used to help with building your business?
I did use flyers for residents, but when I went into commercial cleaning, I would ask friends and network connections and make contact with decision makers from there. I did not use a formal marketing strategy. The majority of my business was word-of-mouth. Once I obtained a contract with my first commercial client, I was able to demonstrate my commitment to my business and theirs. I made sure that my service was excellent and that my cleaning could not be compared to anyone else. They would always recommend me to their colleagues at other offices and locations. As people continued to connect and comment on how great my service was, my business grew in direct relation to the promotions by others.

What are 3 books that you recommend for success in your industry?

- *10 Mistakes People Make in the Cleaning Industry* – Cissy Agurs
- *The Janitorial Contractors Bible* – Robert Jack Kravitz
- *Multi Unit Leadership: The 7 Stages of Building High-Performing Partnerships and Teams* – Jim Sullivan.

If there was one thing you may have done differently in your industry when you got started, what would it have been?

I would have had a business plan and a coach. Having a solid business plan would have afforded me the opportunity to see where some of my potentially challenging areas were and to plot a plan for growth for each aspect of my business. Having a coach would have given me the chance to have a real person to guide and share with me as I learned to make decisions and understand how the business worked.

What is your favorite quote?

"Vision is the art of seeing what's invisible to others. So don't allow those who don't see what you see to break your focus. Don't look to the left. Don't look to the right. Stay focused on what God has for you and all will Be WELL!" —Taurea V. Avant

Special thanks to the following:

Jackie Staton
E2C Solutions HR Consulting
Facebook.com/E2CSbyJai

Sharon Allen
Next Level Consulting Service Business Consultant - Personal Coaching
Facebook.com/Next-Level-Consulting-Services-LLC

Melvina D. Crawl, CEO
Business Consulting & Advisor

Premier Elite Solutions, LLC
Facebook.com/PremierEliteSolutionsLLC

Denise Foulks
Neece's Necessities Jewelry Designer
Facebook.com/NeecesNecessities

Flora Ingram
Flora's Painting Home & Business improvements
Facebook.com/FlorasPainting

Charlene Lee
Benefits Assistance Management Financial Advisor
Facebook.com/BenefitsAssistanceManagement

Ayelech Mackey
Bookkeeping
Total Tax and Financial Services CPA
Facebook.com/TotalTaxandFinancialServices

Dr. Sonja Stribling
Next Level Living 7
Facebook.com/DrSonjaStribling

Derek Atwell
Owner
Derek Atwell CPA, PLLC
Facebook.com/Derekatwell

Troy Conway

Industry - Music Industry
Instagram.com/TroyBConway
Facebook.com/TroyBConway
Periscope.tv/TroyBConway
Twitter.com/TroyBConway
Linkedin.com/in/TroyConway
www.TroyBConway.com

Troy "DJ Vex" Conway is an author, public speaker, business owner, music producer, DJ, and sound technician. At the young age of 18, he leaped into entrepreneurship when he partnered with his two friends and created a DJ and entertainment company. By his 20th birthday, he had already won first place in a citywide DJ contest hosted by a major radio station in Baltimore, Maryland. As a result of winning the contest, he had the honor of being a live guest DJ on that radio station. It was an honor that he still holds near and dear to his heart.

Growing up, Troy had endless support and encouragement from his mother, Jackie Hendricks, and grandmother, Irene Brown. They encouraged him to always shoot for the stars in his music endeavors. He attended Morgan State University where he would DJ most of the campus parties and produce tracks for local artists. Shortly after his 21st birthday, he married his high school sweetheart, Jia Conway, and they share four beautiful kids: Jazmin, Shyniece, Troy (TJ), and Jaila. His wife and kids became his driving force to become more of a businessman by taking his skillset to another level. He learned that in order to be extremely successful, you must be willing to invest finances and time into developing your mind, business, and technical skills.

Throughout his musical career, he was able to earn very significant income on a part time basis as a DJ, music producer, and co-owner of the company that serviced clients throughout the state of Maryland. With music already being his first love, he discovered that turning passion into a successful business would only equate to pure happiness and an amazing income.

How long have you been in your industry?
I have been in the music industry as a DJ for about three quarters of my life. I remember getting my first paid event as a DJ when I was in the fifth grade. Yes, the fifth grade! I was booked—or should I say, "asked"—by my mom's godmother to DJ her wedding anniversary event at a local hall. I can't remember the amount of years she and her husband were celebrating, but I do remember the nervousness that I had leading up to the moment of placing the needle down on the first record. It was funny too! I didn't have any of the "industry standard" equipment. I had

two mismatched turntables, and one of them was broken. I literally had to turn the record with my hand until the motor started. The speakers I had weren't loud enough in my opinion, but surprisingly everyone enjoyed the song selections and didn't seem to mind my shortcomings with the equipment. In fact, I remember someone coming up to me with words of encouragement. He said, "You have a gift, and with the right equipment, you can go far as a DJ." Those words still echo in my head decades later.

Why did you get into your industry?
Music was always a part of my life. I remember going to the record store at the mall for hours while other kids would be in the arcade playing games like PAC-MAN. I would lean up against the counter and watch the store DJs spin records for hours. I would listen to the different styles and combinations of music that they would put together. I was fascinated with the fact that two songs could be manipulated by adjusting the pitch and tempo in order to blend them together so that there is no dead space in between changing songs. In addition to that, I fell in love with the idea of moving a record back and forth with my hand to create a completely different sound that you would not hear if you simply let it play. The sound I'm referring to is known as scratching. After scratching and destroying a few of my grandmother's records on the stereo deck in the basement, I saved my money and purchased my first two records: "The Show" by Doug E. Fresh and "Paid In Full" by Eric B. & Rakim. At that point, all I wanted for holidays and special occasions was money for records or some form of DJ equipment. While in middle/high school, I would create mixed tapes to sell to the students. I used that money to reinvest in more records and equipment. From the mixed tapes, I was able to DJ birthday parties for students and small school functions. Fast forward years later, I joined in partnership with two close friends who were also DJs, and we started a DJ company shortly after my 18th birthday. The company was called, Street Music Entertainment. The company grew to more than ten DJs who would be booked for gigs all over Maryland and D.C. for a span of three years.

When it comes to being an entrepreneur, what do you love most about it?

I love the idea of being my own boss. The idea of having control of my income means a lot to me in providing for my family. Having a job is a blessing, and I'm grateful for every job that I have had, but I also know the feeling of wondering if my hours were going to get cut, which would decrease the amount of my paycheck. I know the feeling of going through a company merger and buyout, wondering if my position was secure or if I would be one of the ones who would be phased out. As a husband and father of four, I know the importance of having additional streams of income flowing into the household in the event that one of the sources runs dry. Being an entrepreneur allows me to have some sense of security in this unstable economy. There's a great feeling associated with being able to create your own opportunities and destiny. As a DJ, I can book a certain amount of events in order to reach my financial goals. In addition to those, being an entrepreneur gives me the freedom to plan my own schedule. To me, the worst feeling in the world is wanting to do something or go somewhere only to have my supervisor tell me that I can't get off. That is a sure way to get my blood boiling. Imagine a very special event for a loved one is taking place, but you can't go because someone else says, "No!"

What would you consider the pros about being in your industry?

Being a DJ has tons of items on the "pros" column. The connections created just from one event can open major doors. For example, I recall providing live sound for an event of highly connected and successful network marketers. Just from that one event, I met at least seven people who booked me for their personal events from family reunions to weddings. One event isn't just one event. One event can lead to so many other events a person can lose count. In fact, most of my events were booked from someone who attended an event that I provided music for. In addition to the connections, you get to travel and see the world. Some DJs in the industry have tour schedules set up like rock stars. The majority of the time, the fee for your travel is added into your booking fee. Isn't that amazing? Another great thing about this industry is how easy technology has made it for people to get started with little or no skill. As long as you have a great personality and know what the hottest songs are, you're in business. Today's technological advances have created equipment that will basically mix the music for you once you program it. There are also companies that will lease equipment or allow you to "play as you pay" so you can have the gear you need to earn income while making reasonably low monthly payments. This is a major plus as I remember it felt like it took years to get all of the equipment I needed to be successful.

Were you required to make any financial and/or time investments to get started?
When I got started back in the late 1980s, I had to invest basically every dollar I got—along with financial contributions of family—to get the equipment and music that was required to be successful. A set of turntables cost $1000, a mixer was $300, the amp and speakers about $600, and records were anywhere from $3.99 to $10.99 apiece. There were no "play as you pay" companies during that time. It was either payment in full, or the gear would have to go on layaway. Now, there are companies that will send you the required equipment up front and take low monthly payments. Also, technology has changed the way music is played. No longer do you need to invest in tons of expensive records; in most cases, a song can be purchased and downloaded for about 99 cents. Just this alone will save a DJ tons of money to create more profit. There is a time investment as well. Time spent supplying music for an event can vary, and the majority of it will be in the evening and night time—which is perfect for people who work, attend school, or have other obligations during the day. Time investment is also needed in developing and sharpening skills and music knowledge. According to alltherighttunes.com, "a full-service DJ/Entertainment company will normally invest 12 to 30 hours to your special event, but it may appear that you are only paying for 4 hours. Consultations, music purchasing and editing, preparation, set-up, and tear-down, education, and other business related endeavors add up to the overall success of your special occasion." I used to spend at least 3 hours per day doing just that. However, if you're a music lover, the time will fly by.

What are the statistics of success in your industry?
According to dj-rankings.com, there are at least 1,261,314 "registered" professional DJs in the world with 20,769 new DJs in 2015. I know this may seem like a lot, but factor this in globally. There are so many events taking place per day and not enough DJs to fulfill the bookings. Many times people have to resort to other means of providing music or live sound for their events. I think it's safe to say that many of us have attended events in which a CD or MP3 player was the DJ. I can't count the number of times I had to tap into my connection of DJs to cover bookings simply because people just couldn't find an available DJ. With so many events and the rates that a DJ can charge, many people can create full-time income based on their personal goals.

What is the average income in your industry?
The average income for a hired DJ by a radio station is $32.50 per hour. Keep in mind, this is for someone who has a set schedule and company rules to follow with the possibility of termination at any time. However, self-employed DJs can earn some really great income. According to alltherightunes.com, "Rates for the DJ/Entertainment industry vary greatly. The income range is from $350 to over $5,000 with an average of $1,200 for a 4-hour booking." With numbers like that, you can easily see how the income can add up quickly. Keep in mind, this is only for one event. Imagine multiple events taking place during the same week or even the same day. In some cases, one or two booked events per day will generate more income than the average person earns in a full 40-hour work week. Let's look at the math on the lower end. Three events at $350 in seven days will create $1,050. Multiply that by 52 weeks in a year is $54,600. Now, income does vary based on personal income goals and work ethic, but the income potential is limitless.

When it comes to success in your industry, what are 3 main tips you would give to those interested in doing what you do?
The average income for a successful DJ in the industry is about $350-$500 per hour. With that said, not everyone will achieve the average income. I just have to be honest. There are many

factors that will dictate your income, such as clientele, talent, skill set, crowd following, quality, and worthiness. These three tips should be helpful in reaching the average and beyond:

- Be willing to study the industry. There is so much more to being a DJ than just playing a hot song. Understand that you will be responsible for people having a great time. As a DJ, it's your responsibility to make people feel good emotionally while they are in your presence. That's not to put pressure on you, but to get you to understand that taking the time to study the industry will allow you to be prepared.

- Be prepared. This is basically self-explanatory, but vital to your success. Taking the time before your event to carefully plan out your mix set and music selections will make a world of difference in your performance. Spend time putting the best song selections together so that you won't have to spend time searching for the next tune to keep people moving. Also, spend time working on your vocal presence. I've notice from personal experience that proper microphone work will elevate a good DJ to a great DJ.

- BE EARLY! Unlike many things in life that people can get away with being a few minutes late, being a DJ isn't one of them. Give yourself more than enough time to arrive at your event, setup, test, and troubleshoot any possible problem areas. I learned this the hard way in my earlier days as a DJ. I would arrive and have just enough time to setup, but not enough time to test and troubleshoot. Most of the time, there weren't any issues and I was fine, but there were times that I needed an extra 30 minutes or so to resolve surprise problems. Keep in mind things will not always go smoothly, but if you give yourself more than enough time to resolve unplanned issues, you will in most cases have a great performance.

When actively working in your industry, what does a day (week) look like for you?
The day in the life of a DJ in my opinion is great, especially if you love music, people, and money. There really is no set schedule

49

because there is always an event or gig that can be booked every day. I recall a week where I did a football party Monday, Jazz event Tuesday, rested Wednesday, private fundraiser Thursday, night club Friday, wedding Saturday, and a birthday party Saturday night. Now, there were a lot of different factors for each event that made it possible. For some, I didn't have to take all of my equipment. For one, I only needed to take my music selections. During the day or down time, I would research music and practice on my skills for the next gig. It didn't seem like work because I would have been listening to music and mixing songs in the basement anyways. The thought that doing what I love could generate additional income to help out with the bills was motivation for my tired days. Other spinoff items such as T-shirts, personally produced music, and personally promoted events would also occupy my thoughts and preparation. I learned that there were other ways to create income while performing at an event, so I would take time to make sure I had some kind of item to offer the client and guests. I have had events of my own that generated some great additional income as well, so taking time to event plan would, on occasion, find its way into my day.

Do you have a mentor?
I don't have a mentor, but there were several people that I would study and build my business around. One was a local DJ I had the opportunity to work with at one of the record stores in Baltimore. This guy literally performed at events all of the time from clubs, to parties, and eventually the radio. By studying him, I found that there were 4 steps to being a great and successful DJ.

1. **Take pride in your craft and skills.** Every day, you should do something to be better than you were yesterday. This is the reason that I would spend hours in the basement sharpening my skills. I knew that I was the product and wanted to be the best product that I could offer my clients. Sure, there were DJs who were more popular and even more skilled than I was, but one thing I knew for sure was there were more events than DJs. As I worked on getting to

the top level, I knew I had to be the best at my level so that people would keep booking me for events.

2. **Know your limits**. The worst thing I feel that a DJ can do is book an event that doesn't line up with their personal, moral, or spiritual beliefs. To take an event just for the money while you have personal reservations will show in the performance. I see it all of the time. For example, if you don't do drugs, why would you book an event knowing that there will be drug usage? Stay true to yourself and trust that there is enough to go around for everybody. Compromising for money, in my opinion isn't a wise decision.

3. **Be self-motivated**. For the most part, you have to do something in order to get something. You have to get out there and let people know what you do and be willing to show them. This can be in the form of a brief sample of your mixing, videos, or previous gigs, or even offer an invite for someone to be a personal guest to your next event. There is no room for procrastination and poor work ethic. As the expression goes, "It's grind time!" Your actions will definitely dictate your income in this industry, so get out there and be active. Trust me, the rewards are great!

4. **Don't be afraid to step back so that you can jump forward**. This is for the client and you. By all means, I am not saying to sell yourself short, but sometimes it may be in your best interest to offer a discount to get an event that you know has the potential to generate multiple events of equal or higher value. I remember doing a wedding for free. Yes, I said free. I only made them pay for my gas. To some, this may be foolish and not good business, but I already did my homework on the guest list. I knew that being able to be the DJ for that event would offer me the opportunity to meet people who were affluent with influence. Let's just say my gamble paid off! From that one event, I have clients who booked me for events years and years later. With that said, please

51

make sure that you use wisdom when offering service for free so that you don't sell yourself short.

Has being in your industry helped you to expand to other industries?
Absolutely! Being a DJ has allowed me to meet people in basically any industry you can think of. Keep in mind, people have events and people love to have a good time. I've met people with GEDs to Ph.Ds. This has allowed me to expand into acting in movies, new business ventures in network marketing, and even music production. One time, I was providing live sound for a marketing event, and I met an events promoter. He later invited me to an event as a guest DJ, and I met a very successful business professional in the network marketing industry who I partnered up with months later. The connections created by being a DJ are priceless.

If someone was to come to you for help, what would be the first thing you would tell them in regards to getting started in your industry.
I had several people come to me about getting started as a DJ, and the first thing I tell them all is to think about why you want to do it. Is it for the love of music and bringing joy to those who hear you, or is it to earn some great additional income on a part time basis? I feel the why is crucial in helping a person stay on track to reaching their goal. As long as they know why, giving up should never be an option when things don't appear to be going well. From there, the rest is just about making the financial and time investment. That's the easy part, believe it or not.

Outside of working (in your industry) what is your favorite thing to do?
I love spending time with family and friends! Funny thing is, I always find a way to bring music into it! One time, my family was invited to a friend's birthday cookout. I really wanted to stay home a practice my skill, but I also wanted to enjoy the cookout. So, I loaded the back of the SUV with some equipment and off we went. When we arrived, I heard a small radio playing. Little did they know, it was about to go down! They laughed as I carried in the equipment, but once I played the first song, we partied for

about five hours. I had no hidden motive to gain gigs from doing that—it really was for the love of music and having a great time. Needless to say, I ended up with gigs by default and a few dollars in tips that was forced on me from those in attendance. Outside of music and spending time with family, I enjoy reading, writing, personal development, traveling, and anything related to sports. Go Baltimore Ravens!

Do you provide coaching or resources to anyone who wants to further educate themselves in your industry?

I do not have any formal coaching service as of yet, but I am always open to guide and assist anyone looking to get into this industry. I feel that I have the blue print and connections to get someone off to a great start. I can also teach the required skills to take a person from just playing songs to creating a full mix set that will be sure to rock the house! I had someone reach out to me on social media who was looking to start a DJ business, but didn't have any idea of what to do. I set up a time to meet with him at a local Starbucks and gave him detailed information and resources that he would need to get off to a successful start. I also had plenty of people who wanted to learn the skill of blending two songs together in which I've taken the time to teach them how. I do believe in the near future that I will create some form of training system to teach others how to get into the industry and how to be successful in it.

Is there anything you don't necessarily love about the industry?

Just like any other industry, there are some downsides. The time spent away from family and friends can be a bit much at times, but I found a solution to ease this. I try to book events that give me room to invite family and friends at times so that I can spend time with them while having fun, doing what I love, and earning some money. There's nothing like making money while having fun with loved ones! Another downside for some is you have to put in the work. This is not like a job where you have a set schedule. You have to be willing to promote yourself in order to get booked. However, once you develop your skills, build your resume and clientele, you should be in position to book events from an event. As you can see, it's not much that I don't love about the industry. With a few tweaks here and there, the minor things can be resolved.

What favorite marketing strategies have you used to help with building your business?

1. **Referral Program.** Good old fashioned word-of-mouth works like a charm. A referral from a friend can open a door with many more doors of opportunity behind it. People trust their friends and family, so make sure to let everyone know that they should contact you when they require a DJ. I would always make sure to offer a discount or some form of appreciation for the referral.
2. **Networking.** I would make sure that I network with other DJs. I can't count the times I've outsourced an event to another DJ or picked up an event that another DJ couldn't take. Building positive relationships is vital in this industry. Don't be afraid to connect with others.
3. **Loyalty program.** I would always reach out to my clients and offer some form of discount or appreciation for continued business. I would let them know that bigger rewards come with more event bookings and they can build up to the potential of 50% off! It's like having a punch card. The more punches, the bigger the reward.

What are 3 books that you recommend for success in your industry?

1. *Last Night a DJ Saved My Life: The History of the Disc Jockey* - Bill Brewster and Frank Broughton
2. *How to DJ Right: The Art and Science of Playing Records* - Bill Brewster and Frank Broughton
3. *How to Win Friends & Influence People* - Dale Carnegie

If there was one thing you may have done differently in your industry when you got started, what would it have been?

I would have believed in myself more and pushed myself to go "all in" full-time. Being a DJ on a part-time basis is great. It's on my own terms and time, but back in the earlier days of my career, I wish I would have viewed the industry as my only way. It's what I love to do, and the income potential is ridiculous! When I look at the list of the highest paid DJs in the world, I find myself in a daze. The top 12 DJs in 2014 pulled in well over $250 million with Calvin Harris earning an astronomical $66 million by himself. It's never too late! It's time to make that list!

What is your favorite quote?
"If you can do something you love and enjoy doing, it's like getting paid twice." —Andy Strickland

Special Thanks to the following:

Dr. Jia R. Conway
Author, Speaker, Coach, Mentor, CEO
Changing From The Inside Out
Facebook.com/jiarconway

Phyllis Trafton
Women's Mentor, Author, CEO
The Overcomers Network
Facebook.com/phyllistrafton

Delton L. Stanley Sr.
President/CEO
Axiom Nanotech Global
Facebook.com/axiomnanotechglobal

Damon Freeland
Business Owner
Freeland Trucking, LLC
Facebook.com/damonfreeland

Tiffany L. Bethea

Author, Speaker, Coach, Consultant for Spirit-Led
Entrepreneurs
The Tiffany Bethea Group, LLC
Facebook.com/tiffanylbethea

Paul & Destini Duke
Business Owner
PdPhotobooth
Facebook.com/pdphotobooth

Shena Lenea Randolph
Early Childhood Education
Facebook.com/shenarandolph

Marcia Owens Brown
Practice Administrator

Latasha Everett
Healthcare

Jazmin, Shyniece, Troy, & Jaila Conway
Students

**Jackie & David Hendricks, Irene Brown, Fred Crosby, Hope
Garnette, Olen McCardell, Lanette Parson**

Rebecca Powell

Industry - Food & Business Consulting
Instagram.com/RP3Marketing
Facebook.com/rp3marketing
Persicope.tv/rpowell916
Twitter.com/rpowell916
Google.com/+/rp3marketinggroup
Linkedin.com/in/Rebecca-Powell-a2634265
www.RP3marketing.com

Rebecca RP3 Powell is a single mom, friend, mentor, chef, and consultant. Since 2011, she started her journey as a business woman and entrepreneur. With fifteen years of working different jobs that helped her gain the knowledge, but not the income that she wanted, she was able to take her game to the next level. Years of putting in the time and yet to see any results, she finally had a breakthrough in 2010, when she worked as an intern for a consulting company. And from that moment forward, that same opportunity would open the doors to a world that would give her the chance to impact the industry of the consulting world.

Life will throw you a curve ball, but it is how you use the bat that will determine how far the ball goes.

How long have you been in your industry?
In 2009, I started my career as a non-paid intern for a professor who ran his own consulting company in the food industry. This gave me the opportunity to learn from working with several clients, which helped me gain the foundation of what a successful business consultant needed to make it in this industry—mainly good communication skills. The more I work with each client, the more I gain experience as each client is unique in their own way. Although I have gained a great deal of experience in seven years, I think it is important to strive to continue to learn and evolve. This has given me the confidence to go out on my own as a successful business woman.

Why did you get into your industry?
At first, I entered into this profession because I loved the restaurant industry, but I knew that I didn't want to be in the kitchen. I chose the business/food consulting because I found that I could see potential problems and was able to create solutions fairly quickly. As a result, it seemed to have an impactful result for the client. After doing some research on what it takes to own a successful restaurant, I wanted to dive in deeper. According to the Bureau of Labor and Statistics, "A recent Cornell University study showed the number of restaurants failing in the first year is closer to 60 percent, and while this may still seem high, statistics need to be examined in

context to be fully understood. Restaurants are actually no more risky than any other new business." There are common mistakes made by restaurants that are avoidable and can cause their facility to be shut down. For example, repeated health and safety codes, trends, regulations, labor laws, consumer needs, and a variety of other changes in the industry can impact their business.

The business/food consulting industry also gave me opportunities to tap into a variety of niche markets. I work with restaurants, chefs, catering companies, event planners, non-profits, law firms, small businesses, corporations, and start-ups, just to name a few. Some common mistakes in the food industry are a lack of experience, ineffective employee management, poor location, and inconsistent customer service. Further, balancing the demands of the business—which is very time consuming—and personal life can be quite challenging.

As a business/food consultant, I aspire to bring the client current and accurate knowledge, proven skills, experience, and processes designed to improve their situation. This includes sharing my experience in human resources, administration, health and sanitation, food cost, menu planning food presentation, food quality, leadership and development, marketing, branding, etc. I have the ability to combine all of my skills and talents together to execute several phases that allows me to correct each problem identified at the time of our consultation and further into the project.

My formal education taught me how to deal with both sides of the restaurant industry, but the hands-on experience gave me even more. Knowing that I am providing the client with the proper tools and strategies to use once I have finished the project shows me that together, we have been successful in enhancing a profitable business.

This is where my passion began to evolve in the world of food consulting. There is a high demand for my profession, especially in today's economy, to help business owners save their investments, time, and energy.

When it comes to being an entrepreneur, what do you love most about it?

I love that I am able to bring out my unique gifts and talents to the surface to shine. It has been the most rewarding thing I have done not only for myself, but for my son as well. I have been able to show him that there is more than one way to showcase his talents. There is no greater reward to me than knowing I was able to help someone find their own talent and use it to develop and implement it in their business.

Being an entrepreneur has allowed me to be myself. I have learned so much about how to progress as a business woman. I don't think I would have appreciated this if I had taken a different path. It has helped me to believe in myself and grow a thick skin. Life has thrown me situations that I thought may have been the demise of my business. Then, when I least expected it, I was blessed with an opportunity to keep moving forward. That tells me that I am in the right business for the right reasons— helping others.

I see situations and people as life lessons. Out of every one, I learn and grow as a woman and business owner. During difficult times when things just don't seem to be going the way I want, I remind myself that I have a burning desire for success and that my goals and dreams are worth fighting for. I now look forward to challenges for inspiration to keep moving forward.

What would you consider the pros about being in your industry?

The pros about being in the consulting industry are that I can offer services to a diversified clientele. As a consultant, I bring my knowledge, skills, experience, and developing systems to improve the client's profit margins.

Companies are looking to reduce their cost in overhead or their lack of experienced employees to execute the needs and goals of the company. When companies find themselves in this situation, this is where the decision has to be if hiring a consultant is the right fit for their business. Not only is hiring a consultant cost-effective for a business, but it also gives the business owner the opportunity to leverage knowledge.

As a food consultant, there are three things I know consumers look for when they go out to dine—whether it's fine dining or fast-food: 1) Customer service, 2) Amazing food, and 3) Experience.

As a consultant, I also get to look at the details of how the business is running from the standpoint of government and regulatory compliance, research and development, new product development, cost reduction, general/turnaround management, consumer recipe development, and the list goes on and on. When a restaurant owner goes into business, they tend to look at the bigger picture and leave out some of the finer details, which then lead to having to close their business sooner than they expected.

So the pro in food consulting is that as long as there are business owners, there is always need for my services.

Were you required to make any financial and/or time investments to get started?
I love getting asked the question if I was required to make any financial and/or time investment to get started in my business. No, I wasn't required, but I made the decision to invest time and money to see the vision of having my own company come to life.

When I first started out in the industry, I donated a lot of my time in order to gain the experience and skills I would need in order to branch out on my own someday. There were periods that I had to sacrifice time with my son, celebrations, holidays, events, and a social life because I was investing time into myself in order to develop as a consultant. These are some of the time sacrifices that I had to make at the beginning with different phases of my business. My time investment shifts and adjusts to adapt to the needs of the business.

My financial investment as a beginning student in the world of business consulting was very minimal, simply because I was in the learning stages of the industry. However, I didn't allow that to stop me from investing in myself. The library was a great starting point to further my knowledge on the consulting and food industry.

When setting up my office space, I needed the basic office supplies: pen, paper, folders, binders, dividers, and envelopes. Inexpensive stores to purchase these items are (Dollar Tree, 99 Cent Store, Wal-Mart) great places to shop for supplies and they won't break the bank. The average that I spent in office supplies, in the first 90-120 days was approximately $50.00.

In the beginning I was trying to budget my expenses, but I needed a laptop, Wi-Fi, a desk, a chair and other items that could give me a space to work from home. I purchased a used laptop from a friend for $150 to get me by. I would go to places that offered free Wi-Fi, and I went to garage sales to find my desk and chair that cost me $80. I made it work at the beginning, and I didn't need to have fancy things just yet.

When it came to my marketing, I reached out to my fellow classmates that were in the graphics and marketing department in the university I was attending. The students in these departments had to pick up projects for certain classes to obtain experience, and I was able to get my marketing material done at a low cost. I would trade work for work, but if I'd had to pay out of pocket, it would have cost me on an average from $500-$1000. I would cater parties or events for them to give me experience, but it also helped me get the work I needed done. It was a win-win.

I had some travel expenses, meals, lodging, networking events, and licensing fees that I paid for over time ($1000-$2000). What I did was prioritize in the order of importance and cost so I could make sure that I had the things that I needed and budgeted for. When I had a little bit of money coming in, I could put it into my account so I could then reinvest it into my business.

What are the statistics of success in your industry?

The statistics of success in the consulting in general vary widely because consulting has many avenues that one person might take. For the food consulting, there is not a lot of information because this branch of consulting has developed in recent years, which means that there is a lot of room for growth for those of us getting started.

According to a 2016 report from New Geography, "In the past decade, businesses in the professional and technical services sectors have been increasingly hiring businesses and consultants from outside of their own companies to handle departmental work such as advertising, payroll, and human resources. In 2013, the company's revenue exceeded 32 billion U.S. dollars – almost a third of which came from consulting."

What is the average income in your industry?

In this industry, the beauty about this business is that you can have multiple projects going on at the same time. But in reality, price is based on the value of the consultant. I take a look at the client's budget to determine what they can afford. I won't charge a client $7,500 when they only have monthly sales of $15,000. Now, if the client I am working with is looking to take their business from $100,000 to $300,000, then I look at putting them on a six-month contract so we can work in phases to achieve the client's goal.

When it comes to success in your industry, what are 3 main tips you would give to those interested in doing what you do?

Be passionate about what you do, be prepared to make mistakes, and become the best student of the industry.

Being passionate about what you do is very important because when you are trying to help others get out of a negative situation that they may have caused for themselves, you have to be able to help them without passing judgment. Sometimes I see some of these clients that honestly had misguidance or lack of experience, and they just need help to get them on the right path.

Knowing that I can be that person to help them with that change makes me feel like I was able to make a difference.

Mistakes are going to happen, so expect them to happen. I am already letting you know that you will make mistakes, and you want to make mistakes and learn from them. You cannot move forward in this industry without making mistakes. I can tell you when I first came to this industry as an intern, I made plenty of mistakes, but had the right mentor to teach me to learn from those mistakes. One thing you must learn is to not be afraid to ask questions. Always something with you to take notes always. I can tell you that there is nothing worse than coaching/training someone that isn't taking notes, and then later on comes to ask me a question about something from earlier on. Take notes, and ask questions. When you make a mistake, ask how it could have been prevented or done differently, and ask for guidance. Get counsel so you can be prepared to handle the situation if you encounter it again.

A student is always learning. Immerse yourself in as much information you can regarding the food industry, restaurants, cooking, food, nutrition, consulting, leadership, management, coaching, administration, etc. Always be in learning mode in order to gain as much knowledge as you can in order to master your talents and craft. If you are blessed with an amazing mentor, cherish that relationship and guidance, because those mentors don't come that often. Mentors are a wealth of information and experience, and there is no price that you can put on the education that they can provide for you.

When actively working in your industry, what does a day (week) look like for you?
When actively working in consulting, I have what I call admin days and field days. My admin days are the days that I work from my home office. They don't always look the same, but I try to keep them similar to stay on top of things.

- **Admin day**: Set up appointments with clients or potential clients for my field days, review contracts, follow up on emails, research, set up meetings or

trainings, work with team members, marketing, call contractors and set up appointments if needed, and/or pick up any products.
- **Field day:** Meet with clients, consultations with new clients, meet with contractors, deliver tools or materials, do walk-through of facilities, review reports, review phases with clients, and work on-site with existing clients if needed.

This of course varies depending on the amount of projects I have going on at one time, how big or small the project is, and how many team members I have working with me on the project.

Do you have a mentor?

Merriam-Webster Dictionary defines a mentor as someone who teaches or gives help and advice to a less experienced and often younger person.

For me the word mentor has had a different meaning, simply because I have been blessed with an amazing duo of mentors. I would be remised if I did not say thank you to Mr. Samuel Bean and Mrs. Kim Bean, because they invested and believed in me before I did. When you have a mentor or mentors who can guide you in business, life situations, parenting, etc., that is a blessing and something that cannot be taken for granted. They both have guided me and directed me to grow into the business woman I have become. Even during the times that I thought I was ready to throw in the towel or didn't want to get out of my comfort zone, they kept pushing me. Learning to trust in someone else to lead me to the success I wanted to achieve because they have already accomplished it has been the smartest things I could have ever done. There are no words on how eternally grateful I am for them.

With that said, here is some advice that I received from the amazing duo:

1. Start with the intent to listen and build your bullet points around the need of the clients.

2. Know what you are talking about, and if you don't know, don't be afraid to tell the client that you will get back to them.
3. Have humility; have a humble heart and spirit.
4. Self-programming—what type of information are you processing through to your brain.
5. Have a great attitude; be happy all the time.
6. Forget about fear and push forward.
7. Don't be out of focus because it just gets blurry.
8. Repeat a person's name at least five times within a conversation.
9. Within the first 30 seconds, establish a rapport with the client.
10. Pay attention to what is going on with the person via body language.
11. Learn about whom you are working with, build trust, and build a relationship.
12. Never quit, never quit, your dreams are too big to quit.

Has being in your industry helped you to expand to other industries?
Having the opportunity to be in the food industry has opened many doors for me to expand into other industries:

1. Catering
2. Wedding
3. Business
4. Meal prepping
5. Event coordination;
6. Worked alongside professional chefs
7. Commodities distribution
8. Health and wellness industry
9. Specialty food and nutrition
10. Business/wedding consulting

If someone was to come to you for help, what would be the first thing you would tell them in regards to getting started in your industry?
The first thing I would tell them is, "Don't quit your job." Too often we get excited to start a new venture and want to clock out

of our current jobs to focus full time on our dreams, but it doesn't work that way because the bills still have to be paid. Trust me, I am guilty of doing this, and I learned the hard way. Having income coming in will help with building your business and giving you leverage to invest in your business.

Next, do your homework. What is it about the food consulting that really intrigues you? Is it that you want to know why some restaurants have more customers during certain hours than others? Or why is the employee retention better in some restaurants than others? What does a profitable menu look like? What does quality food look and taste like? These are some questions that I might ask to find the reason the person wants to dive into the industry.

Then, I would ask how much time and work can they put in. When starting your own business, it takes a lot of time and work. Especially in the food industry, the hours of operation for restaurants are different than typical office hours, and some projects may require travel, while others may require research and development.

These are just a few things to give a person an idea of what it looks like when getting into a business. Any industry is going to require work, and with hard work comes great success.

Outside of working (in your industry) what is your favorite thing to do?
Outside of food consulting, my favorite thing to do is be a mom. Of course, I enjoy working out, hanging out with my friends, eating (of course), cooking, traveling, and enjoying life.

Here is why my favorite thing to do is being a mom—it's not easy, especially being a single mom. It takes a lot of hard work, patience, understanding, sacrifice, love, responsibility, character, faith, change, laughter, sadness, struggle, sleepless nights, exhaustion, decisions, drive, wisdom, mistakes, and I could go on, but I know all you parents know what I am talking about.

With all that being said, it has been the most rewarding thing of all. My son has been the biggest blessing to me. He keeps me accountable and won't allow me to quit because I have given him my word. I love hearing him laugh and sing when he is happy and being around to give him hugs and kisses when he cries. I love the excitement in his voice when he does well in school, the expression on his face when he hit his first home run, and when he hears his favorite song on the radio and dances to the beat. I get to enjoy every special moment. Being a mom isn't easy, but it does have its greatest rewards, and knowing that my decisions will impact someone else's life makes me think twice about what I am going to decide.

Do you provide coaching or resources to anyone who wants to further educate themselves in your industry?
I will provide coaching to anyone who would like to learn about the food business consulting industry. If someone comes to me for coaching on the industry, I will want to highlight their talents, skills, and experience. This will provide me with an idea of where the individual is at and what qualities they bring with them. With there being so many opportunities and different areas in the food consulting business, it's a matter of matching talent and opportunity in order for it to be a fulfilling experience.

I am creating a program so individuals can get some background knowledge on the business and industry itself. My goal will be to adapt an internship program for students with seminars, training classes, and workshops in order to have this industry grow more.

Is there anything you don't necessarily love about the industry?
Something that I don't necessarily love about this industry is that you are working with different personality types, and I have had to learn how to work with all kinds of personalities. I have had clients will utilize the tools given to them but then slowly sink into the bad habits that got them into the situation they were previously in. As the consultant, this can sometimes be frustrating because it's like starting from scratch, so I have to

help them get back on track. Then I have my clients that want to do so many things that they can't start with one, and it can become overwhelming because I have had to learn when to slow them down to get them focused on one idea at a time. This industry does take a lot of time and sacrifice, which means I have had to give up on some things in order to be able to invest time into my business and career. There is a learning curve of balancing family and business, and the pressure does hit when one isn't getting the attention that it should. It is a learned love of the industry, but it comes with time.

What favorite marketing strategies have you used to help with building your business?

1. Networking, networking, networking. I cannot emphasize enough how networking has helped with expanding my business. I was taught early on in my career that it was important to get myself out into the business world and meet individuals in different areas of business. Now with technology you can basically find different networking events on many social media sites hosted by different markets of business. The events hosted by different areas of businesses have allowed me the opportunity to meet individuals in areas of business that I may typically not have tapped into.

2. Word of mouth/Referrals are very important. There is nothing like someone referring your services to colleagues, friends, and family. It is very important for me to deliver to the client, because if the client is happy, I know he is going to let everyone he/she knows the results we were able to achieve together, but if I don't deliver, they will make sure to let everyone know that as well. Being a small business owner and starting in my area, it is very important for me to make sure that the customer gets excellent customer service, because in return they will make sure that they return the favor by sending me business.

3. Social media is a great tool for free marketing. As a small business owner, this is great because you are able to use different social media platforms to get your name out there. One thing I can suggest when using social media is to get some help or research on how to use it resourcefully so that it will be profitable and it isn't wasting time. This is where I learned early on that I was so focused on getting things on social media that I would let other things fall through the cracks, so I had to seek out some tools to help me how to become productive in this area.

What are 3 books that you recommend for success in your industry?

1. *Consulting to the Rescue* - Rebecca Powell
2. *The 7 Habits of Highly Effective People* - Stephen R. Covey
3. *Think and Grow Rich* - Napoleon Hill

If there was one thing you may have done differently in your industry when you got started, what would it have been?

I would have known what I wanted to do with my talent a lot sooner. Trying to focus on other things and not focusing on the talent that I had already within myself wasn't wasted tim, but prolonged my journey. I needed to know that quality and value I had and needed to run with it.

What is your favorite quote?

"You gain strength, courage, and confidence by every experience in which you really stop to look fear in the face. You are able to say to yourself, 'I lived through this horror. I can take the next thing that comes along.'" —Eleanor Roosevelt

Special thanks to the following:

Rebecca Carlson
Executive Chef

Debbie Branch Edwards
Cosmetics

Mark R. Kowalewksi
Owner & Immigration Attorney
Accent Legal & Accent Legal

Nicki Crapotta
Owner/Personal Trainer
The Health & Beauty Project

Etzel Ecleston
Makeup Artist

Brandon Manning
Freelance Photographer

Josh Fields
Owner of Direct Designs

Scott Cartwright
Author and Coach
"The Hoss Transformation eBook"

Michelle Curran
Owner
Mitchies Munchies

Tony Ferriera
Founder at A & D Designs, Publisher at L'Vegue, Publisher at Infinity Business Magazine, Founder at A & D Designs, Publisher at L'Vegue, and Publisher at Infinity Business Magazine

Jackie Nakapaahu
Owner
Sa'Vory De'Lites Catering

Debra Akeson
Farmers Insurance Agent

Deborah Morris
World Financial Group

Amanda Laubegayer Belt
Arbonne Consultant

Michelle Dorado
Owner
Essence Hair Salon

Fieuy Doral
Consultant and Jeweler
Premier Designs

Stephanie Morin Sherwood
The Tapestry Network
Founder

Michelle Harrington
Real Estate Agent

Alex Treglazoff-Dober
Owner
Alex With Angels

Denean R. Ambersley

Industry - Property Management
Instagram.com/DeneanAmbersley
Facebook.com/Denean.R.AmbersleyServiceToManyLeadsToGr
eatness
Twitter.com/DeneanRA
Google.com/+DeneanAmbersley
Linkedin.com/in/denean-r-ambersley-0547b817
www.DeneanRAmbersley.com

Denean R. Ambersley is an author, international public speaker, business owner, veteran, and mother. At the young age of twelve, she leaped into the journey of becoming an entrepreneur by selling local newspapers in Baltimore, Maryland. There she got her first taste of profits, later to only discover that, *"Profits are better than wages. Wages make you a living; profits make you a fortune."*—Jim Rohn.

After attending some college, she left to join the military and discovered that the military provided allowances (extra monies) for housing and food. She had a friend to introduce her to property management in which she purchased multifamily homes, rented them, and always made a profit. Falling in love with providing homes to families, this adventure became her part time business. In order to be successful, you must be willing to invest finances and time into developing your mind, business skills, and technical skills. She took a real estate investment course with Dean Degrazious and Robert Kiyosaki and immediately purchased her first three properties that same year. Denean absolutely believes in taking action! By achieving these amazing milestones, she was able to earn significant income on a monthly basis, better known as passive income. Because of her entrepreneurial spirit, she was able to create a net worth of more than $500,000 within just two years. By providing families with a safe, clean, and comfortable place to live, work, and play, Denean has turned real Estate investing/property management into a full-time source of income, happiness, and a way to provide service to many.

How long have you been in your industry?
I have been in the real estate/residential property management Industry since 1995. I purchased my first home in Killeen, Texas.

Why did you get into your industry?
I always knew I was an entrepreneur, and after consulting with one of my investment brokers, she insisted that I learn to be a real estate investor and property manager. I thought she wanted me to invest in real estate simply for real estate itself. As the years went on and my base of education in the real estate industry grew, I came to better understand the bigger picture of

the world of real estate investing and property management. I got into the industry by purchasing my first residential home, and realized I had to leave that location within the next two years. The property was in a perfect location for military families as it was outside a military installation, so I kept this property and rented it for $300.00 dollars above the mortgage; the learning and profits began.

When it comes to being an entrepreneur, what do you love most about it?

I love being an entrepreneur, because it gives me freedom—freedom to move, work, and provide an excellent product or service to many. As an entrepreneur, I've had the opportunity to travel domestically and internationally. As well as choosing the people I work and partner with, as your own boss, you also have the ability to create your own opportunities by doing things like attending conventions, networking with like-minded people and much more. In doing this, you shape your own destiny. Whenever I travel out of my state, I arrive early and leave later than the scheduled event in that town. This gives me time to see the local sites, shows, and possibly network with new people. You work according to your goals, your timeline, and your availability. Having the ability to dictate when I work, when I'll be in the office, and when I'll be available for meetings is freedom that I simply never want to let go of. If I want to take the afternoon off to play golf, tennis, or attend my local gym, then I can. You can't do that working for someone else. As an entrepreneur, I play while I work. I can honestly say I've wholeheartedly believed in and thoroughly loved every product and service I've produced for my residents. You can help thousands of people who need a place to live, work, and play. I'm very proud that I can solve people's housing problems and make a difference in the process. Solving a problem for someone is the time-honored property management 101 strategy of business. Give people what they need to get over a hurdle, and you'll enjoy success.

What would you consider the pros about being in your industry?

As a residential property manager, my biggest personal pro is putting people in homes. If you learn the ins and outs of property management, you can make money whether the real estate market is going up, down, or sideways. As long as your property is cash flow positive, you can ride out a downturn in the real estate market. If you are ready to become a sophisticated investor and find out how to use the tax codes, legal aspects, and other known advantages, then investing in real estate offers great opportunities. After that, we have residual income and tax advantages, and the residual income *always* supersedes the mortgage. The tax advantages to being a property manager reduce your tax liability significantly. Owning a home, condo, or building can be a great long-term investment, and making an informed decision about how to manage your property is the best way to make the most of it. Using a property manager or becoming a property manager puts a professional on your side to make sure your property is getting the attention and revenue it deserves.

Were you required to make any financial and/or time investments to get started?

It's true—you don't need money down, but I recommend having approximately $10 to $25,000 in available funds and good credit in order to get started. Investing to become a property manager can be obtained in several ways, in which I would like to share three different ways I acquired my properties. As a real estate owner, you can transition from being a resident of your personal property to becoming the property manager of that property. Seeking the right team, such as book keeper/accountant, professional handyman, and real estate attorney is paramount. You also can purchase real estate at a ridiculously low discount, which is known as distressed property. Lastly, you can reach out to transitioning owners who do not want to sell their homes, but would like to profit off them and ask to manage the property while they are away.

What are the statistics of success in your industry?

Operating conditions for the property management industry are expected to remain positive over the next five years, though this will eventually slow. Over the next few years, the value of residential construction is expected to expand rapidly due to improved consumer confidence and low interest rates, causing an increase in the housing stock. As a result, the US homeownership rate is projected to increase, and fewer consumers will therefore require property management services. To combat this, firms are expected to offer more services such as long-term maintenance contracts to attract renters

The property management industry offers third-party or outsourced services to handle the upkeep, maintenance, and tenant relations for property owners or landlords. Demand for industry services relies on how much multifamily residential space (e.g. apartment buildings) and commercial space (e.g. office buildings) is occupied by tenants, which is influenced by the availability and attractiveness of homeownership and general economic activity. The industry grew steadily in the decade prior to the Great Recession and benefited from a trend of property owners outsourcing management services to cut costs and focus on other activities

What is the average income in your industry?

The median annual property manager salary is $88,238 with a range usually between $77,445 and $105,364. However, the salary for someone with the title property manager may vary depending on a number of factors including industry, company size, location, years of experience, and level of education. Our team of certified compensation professionals has analyzed survey data collected from thousands of HR departments at companies of all sizes and industries to present this range of annual salaries for people with the job title property manager in the United States.

When it comes to success in your industry, what are 3 main tips you would give to those interested in doing what you do?

1. Obtain a mentor, this person or persons can walk you through the process of starting your property management business.
2. Work or volunteer part time at a property management company; this will give you experience in this industry.
3. Finally, obtain a good accountant because there are lots of money to be made in this industry, but there are also other financial and tax responsibilities that have to be adhered to.

When actively working in your industry, what does a day (week) look like for you?
A work week, especially the first five days of the week, relate to the overall operation of a property, including rent collection, inspections, maintenance, trash removal, security, and some renovation activities. Industry players may also help manage a property's accounting, but operations related to the transactions of properties or real estate investments are not included in this industry. Other activities include having breakfast with a potential seller or renter, looking at properties listed in the local newspaper or online, reading comparisons in certain zip codes, market analysis, and possibly talking with real estate agents.

Do you have a mentor?
Bottom line, you *need* a mentor, or it could cost you hundreds of thousands of dollars. Do not go at it alone! I have a mentor and have learned much from my main mentor and a host of other consultants. If you want to invest in real estate, you should find a local real estate investment association. There is at least one in each major city, and for sure one in every state. Becoming a member of this association will give you access to agents, brokers, personal sellers/investors, hard money lenders, and a host of sponsors in the real estate environment. They assist you in the local customs of buying and selling real estate.

You might also find your mentor in this real estate investment group. You might find one that will give you consultation on your particular investment without charge. Most would be glad to assist you and help you along.

There are those that might take you by your hand and show you the ropes. If all you want to do is invest in real estate, you do not need a real estate license, but a mentor is still necessary. If you do get a license and you purchase a property from an individual, you would have to make all sort of disclosures. There is nothing wrong with getting a license, however, I found it a little burdensome. You can accomplish the same objective without the real estate license.

There may be times when you would want to hire a real estate agent. Make sure the agent you hire understands that you are an investor and not just a buyer or seller that has emotions attached to the property you are selling or buying.

Has being in your industry helped you to expand to other industries?
Yes, network market and commercial rental properties such as storage units and apartment building ownership are future projects that I am working on.

If someone was to come to you for help, what would be the first thing you would tell them in regards to getting started in your industry.
I would act as a consultant and find out exactly what they want to do and ask them to bring their 5-year plan to our first meeting. Prior to our first meeting, I would ask them to attend a Real Estate Investment Association (REIA) meeting in their local city/state.

Outside of working (in your industry) what is your favorite thing to do?
I am a lady of leisure; I love to spend time with my adult children, travel, hike, go to spin classes, attend networking events, and look at dream homes.

Do you provide coaching or resources to anyone who wants to further educate themselves in your industry?

Yes, I provide coaching on how to start, pick a team of advisors, read and conduct a market analysis, and explain how to select homes to manage. If they are local, I will attend a REIA meeting with them.

Is there anything you don't necessarily love about the industry?

There are some pitfalls to property management, which don't have anything to do with the housing market. Tenants that are served eviction notices, tenants that don't respect your properties, and tenants that become squatters are my three things that I don't like about this business. With this said, background checks are paramount prior to leasing.

What favorite marketing strategies have you used to help with building your business?

I frequently check the property management databases and Department of Housing and Urban Development (HUD) housing databases along with online marketing.

What are 3 books that you recommend for success in your industry?

- *Protect and Enhance Your Estate: Definitive Strategies for Estate and Wealth Planning* - Robert A. Esperti, Renno L. Peterson, and David K. Cahoone
- *The Complete Idiot's Guide to Making Money with Rental Properties* - Brian and Casey Edwards, and Susannah Craig-Edwards
- *Rich Dad's Real Estate Advantages: Tax and Legal Secrets of Successful Real Estate Investors* - Sharon L. Lechter and Garrett Sutton

If there was one thing you may have done differently in your industry when you got started, what would it have been?
Sought out a local mentor, join a local property management association, and hired an accountant to balance my books right away. All these things would have been combined as one.

What is your favorite quote?
"Service to many leads to greatness." —Jim Rohn

Special thanks to the following

Rachel Evans
Certified Health Coach, Speaker, Author
Facebook.com/BoomingHealth4Life

Kidra Fuller
International Distributor
Nucerity International
Facebook.com/Kidra-Nucerity-International-Distributor

Darlene Hagood
Founder, Speaker, Author, Evangelist
Sisters Encouraging Sisters Ministries
Facebook.com/SESMinisties

Dr. Sabrina Moore
Owner, Create A Book Today, Personalized Children's Books

Kadenia Javis
CFO, Accountant, Speaker, Author
Javis Financial Services
Facebook.com/JavisTaxService

Veronica Kinard
Owner/General Manager, Capital City Cougars

Faith Adam
Independent Beauty Consultant, Arbonne
Facebook.com/faith.davina

Sylvia P. Laughlin Ministries
Senior Pastor, Speaker, Leader
World Outreach Christian Life Center, Church Without Walls
Facebook.com/WOCLCM

Brad & Annette Weber
Owners, Manager, SUPERCUTS

Lin P. Johnson
Photographer, Picture This Photography LLC
Facebook.com/lin.pattersonjohnson

Dr. Sharon Cole
CEO, Certified Nurse Practitioner, ELOC, LLC
Consulting and Visiting Nurse Practitioner Services

Michelle McKie Hendley
Owner, Manager, and Acquisitions Consultant
M&M Cleaning Services
Facebook.com/michelle.mckie

Betty Parker, CPLP
President, Speaker, Leader, Certified Leadership Trainer,
Certified Coach
Sharper Development Solutions, Inc.
Facebook.com/SharperDevelopment

Shonda Harrington
Owner, Event Planning and Designer
Anointed Planning and Design, LLC
Facebook.com/Anointed-Planning-and-Designs-Llc

Angela Odom
Owner, Speaker, Author
AMO Consulting Solutions, LLC
Facebook.com/amoconsultingsolutions

Shane Billiot
Owner, Acquisitions, Real Estate Investor
Bayou Billiot Seafood, LLC

Facebook.com/shane.billiot/Bayou Seafood

Chaye Alexandra
Owner, Radio Personality-Music Designer
Chayz Lounge, the Sounds of Smooth R&B and Jazz 24/7
Facebook.com/Chayz.Lounge

Lin Johnson
Independent Distributor, Thirty One Gifts
Facebook.com/lin.pattersonjohnson-31 Gifts

Fisher Properties
President, REI, Speaker, Author, Coach
Fisher Properties Enterprises, Inc.
Facebook.com/fisher.property

Denean The Coffee Queen
Global Business Consultant
Denean's FB Cafe
Facebook.com/deneanthecoffeequeen

Elishea Moore

Industry - Healthy & Wellness
Instagram - @ElisheaMooreFacebook -
Facebook.com/CoachElisheaMoore
Twitter.com/ElisheaMoore
Linkedin.com/in/elishea-hester-moore-a19a587
www.ElisheaMoore.com

Elishea Moore is an author, entrepreneur, empowerment speaker, and minister. She started her journey as a life changer ten years ago when she was given the opportunity to head a women's empowerment group "Soul of a Woman." Elishea learned that in order to be a success you must be of significance in the lives of others. In 2008, she was introduced to the platform of network marketing. After several failed attempts she went on to become a multiple six-figure earner and has been instrumental in helping others do the same.

How long have you been in your industry?
I was introduced to this industry in 2008, eight years ago to be exact.

Why did you get into your industry?
I got into this industry in the beginning to support a friend. I had no interest at all in building a business, as a matter of fact I thought that this industry was really a cop out for people that didn't want to get a "real job" or for scam artists. One day my pastor invited me to an event, and after listening to the stories of success I was finally convinced that this industry might be my only chance. I knew some of the people there that were having success, and I felt like if they could do it I could as well. I was looking for a way to get my life back, so I jumped in and followed everything they told me to do. It wasn't until sometime later that I started seeing major success.

When it comes to being an entrepreneur, what do you love most about it?
I love the fact that I have choices! This was something that I did not have as long as I relied on one source of income or when I was employed by someone else. I felt as though it took away my choice to enjoy life and to enjoy my family because I never had the time to do anything other than work.

What would you consider the pros about being in your industry?
I would consider the pros of network marketing to be limitless income, time, freedom, and the ability to build new relationships.

86

Were you required to make any financial and/or time investments to get started?

Yes. I have been in the industry for a while and have made several different investments in different companies. The maximum investment that I have made was a little over $1,300.00. I would add that with my current company, my initial investment or startup fee was free. I did, however, make a $400 investment on products in the beginning that I now get free every month. When it comes to time, I have invested several hours into my business; I believe that you get out of something only what you're willing to put in. I have made sacrifices of time to build my business, and it has definitely rewarded me back for that.

What is the average income in your industry?

In the industry of direct sales, the averages are very different, a promoter can go from earning $0 to earning six figures or more. Income is based upon the performances of each individual's work.

When it comes to success in your industry, what are 3 main tips you would give to those interested in doing what you do

1. Be consistent. This is one of the hardest things to get a person to do, however, it is the key component to your potential success in this industry.
2. Study. You have to be a student of your field. In this industry, some pursue it with the hopes of becoming rich overnight, and that is so far from the truth. In this industry you're definitely given the opportunity to invest little and earn a lot, but you have to be a willing student of the industry, study, and find a mentor who can help you implement a course of action for your success.
3. Be coachable and teachable, no matter how much you learn or believe that you know. It is almost like cutting off your air passage the moment that you think that you know everything and no one can teach you anything. Every day that we wake up, we are

faced with an opportunity to learn something new, but it is completely up to you.

When actively working in your industry, what does a day (week) look like for you?
I actively work my business everyday however, I have the ability to manage my time. Early mornings are usually set aside for prayer, meditation, and preparing my children for school. It is definitely important to start everyone off in the morning with the right mindset. Then I have time set aside for follow-up appointments that I may have set from the night before with individuals who are interested in my line of work. Being that I work completely from my phone or laptop, I have the freedom to go out and take care of household things, prepare dinner, and finish the evening off with team calls to start new teams in their journey of direct sales.

Do you have a mentor?
Yes, I have a mentor. I believe that every person should have a mentor in business and in life, and some are lucky enough to have a mentor that can mentor them in both, and I was one of those lucky people. There are several principles that my mentor taught me, however, when it came to business, the one thing that I carry with me throughout this journey is how to set short and long term goals. This keeps us from walking around in circles with no sense of direction, and setting goals also keeps you from getting frustrated when you aren't seeing results because the set goals allows you to understand the process.

1. Short term goals—in business I like to set ninety-day goals because the average person can stay consistent ninety days before taking a break. Within these ninety days, your goal has to be realistic, and it does not have to be a major goal. Remember that you are taking a series of short steps in your journey that will ultimately lead you to your big goal.
2. Long term goal: Just like a short term goal, a long term goal must measurable and realistic in the time that is set. With a long term goal, you have a greater amount of time, so this will allow you to achieve

much more. I typically set a long term goal in business as twelve months, and this is because of the industry that I am a part of, you can potentially change the entire course of your life in twelve months if you follow the plan of action you set for yourself.

Has being in your industry helped you to expand to other industries?
Yes, it has opened opportunities for upcoming television projects, magazine write-ups, book collaborations such as this amazing book, I have been asked to sit on support boards and I'm currently working on a partnering with a women charity group to further the education of women and business.

If someone was to come to you for help, what would be the first thing you would tell them in regards to getting started in your industry?
I would tell them to discover their why. I know that some would say that doesn't matter, but I beg to differ. It was my why that kept me focused when I wanted to give up and throw in the towel. Yes, there were day that I was willing to go back and just settle for a full-time job as an accountant, but every time I would look at my children, it reminded me of my why, and that empowered me to shake it off and get back on the playing field. So your why is the first thing you must discover when stepping into entrepreneurship and especially the direct sales industry.

Outside of working (in your industry) what is your favorite thing to do?
Many may not know this about me, but I sing and write music. This is one of my many talents and I enjoy doing it.

Do you provide coaching or resources to anyone who wants to further educate themselves in your industry?
I do not consider myself as a coach. I am, however, a resource center for those who are partnered with me in business.

Is there anything you don't necessarily love about the industry?

Yes. There are several things that I don't like about the industry, however, the one thing that I dislike the most is the lack of unity that I see in this industry as a whole. No matter what company a person represents, I believe we are greater together. I have often found that people feel they will look better if they talk down another person or the products and/or company he or she represents. Well that is so far from the truth, I often refer back to the old movie, *A Miracle on 34th Street*. Santa referred customers to other department stores that were able to service the customers. The department managers of Macy's were upset in the beginning until they realized that the customers appreciated this, and in return it increased the sales of Macy's department stores. In this industry, we must not lose focus on the priority, and that is to build a successful business by having a satisfied customer acquisitions program.

What favorite marketing strategies have you used to help with building your business?

I am a true believer in social media outlets as well as the old fashioned three-foot rule. This rule is a rule known in the network marketing world. Meaning that you don't let a person come within 3 feet of you without connecting with them. As time evolves, our industry has become more computerized, and I believe that is a great thing especially for us mothers. Most people get into this industry for time, freedom, and money so we don't necessarily want to spend time doing things that may not work. Social media and cloud-based technology is the wave of the future; it allows you to work from wherever you are, stay relevant in your business, and keep your target audience engaged in what's taking place with you and the company that you represent. The three-foot rule definitely comes into play when you're out and about and the opportunity to speak with someone arises.

What are 3 books that you recommend for success in your industry?

- *Your First Year in Network Marketing: Overcome Your Fears, Experience Success, and Achieve Your Dreams –* Mark Yarnell and Rene Reid Yarnell
- *Think and Grow Rich* - Napoleon Hill
- *The Richest Man in Babylon* - George S. Clason

If there was one thing you may have done differently in your industry when you got started, what would it have been?
I would have worked harder in my first ninety days and built mass momentum.

What is your favorite quote?
"When you want to succeed as bad as you want to breathe, then you will be successful."—Eric Thomas

Dr. Jasmine Zapata

Industry - Real Estate
Instagram.com/DrJasmineZapata
Facebook.com/DrJasmineZapata
Persicope.TV/DrJasmineZapata
Twitter.com/DrJasmineZapata
Linkedin.com/in/drjasminezapata
www.DrJasmineZapata.com

Dr. Jasmine Zapata, M.D., is a dynamic author, physician, entrepreneur, and motivational speaker from the Wisconsin area with the mission to heal, uplift, and inspire. A main focus for Dr. Jasmine is preventive medicine, which involves looking at upstream factors and social determinants of health outcomes. Interestingly, one of the biggest social determinants of health outcomes is economic stability, and for this reason Dr. Jasmine got involved in real estate in 2013 as a means to achieve personal financial freedom and help others do the same. She is co-founder of Brown Girl Green Money, a national social network of women of color working to achieve financial freedom and inspire each other along the way, and is also a founding partner of the real estate investing company, Emerge Capital Partners. She owns both residential and vacation rental properties and also has experience with low to no money down techniques to get started in the field of real estate. Her unique strategy for investing in real estate currently allows her to live mortgage free while getting *paid* to live in her own home. Overall, Dr. Jasmine is passionate about creating multiple streams of income for herself as well as teaching others how to do the same. Breaking the chains of poverty is a mission Dr. Jasmine is determined to win!

Dr. Jasmine grew up in Milwaukee, Wisconsin, and struggled with financial adversities on and off throughout her childhood. Despite financial difficulties, her parents and grandparents were real estate investors/entrepreneurs and ignited a fire inside of her that would come to burn full force later in her adulthood. Dr. Jasmine received full tuition scholarships to both college and medical school. Dr. Jasmine was high school valedictorian with a 4.0 GPA, a summa cum laude graduate of Marquette University and received multiple honors upon graduation from both college and medical school, all while juggling being a wife, mother, college athlete, and local/international medical volunteer among other things. She also persevered through the sudden death of her 16-year-old brother while she was in college and the extremely premature birth of her daughter while in medical school. Despite those obstacles she decided to never give up on her dreams, clinging to the message her grandfather instilled into her at a very young

94

age. Her current life's mission is to spread the message of hope, strength, and the power to overcome—not only physically, but spiritually, socially, and economically as well. She has a heart for not only helping others, but also for *empowering* others to be able to one day help themselves.

How long have you been in your industry?
I have been in the real estate industry for about 3 years now and have been successful through various techniques of investing (some of which include no money down!). I have been blessed through my real estate endeavors to own a home and live rent free with my tenants paying the mortgage and me pocketing money every month. I started out with a duplex and I now have a vacation property I rent out as well. I am also involved with our family's trust and am currently in negotiation to purchase additional properties. I also just started a real estate investing company with four other young minority entrepreneurs where we pool our money together to invest in real estate. My goal is to invest my money earned as a doctor into opportunities that create multiple, passive streams of income, and real estate has been a way for me to do that. I'm still new to this, and I'm not a millionaire from real estate (yet), but I have lots of helpful tips for those getting started and have big goals and aspirations for my future!

I also talk to kids about real estate, entrepreneurship, reaching their dreams, and being their own boss. I have been doing this motivational speaking since I myself was a teenager.

I have been in the medical field and studying ways to prevent death and disease for more than ten years. How real estate connects with me being a doctor is this: one of the biggest determinants of health outcomes is poverty. It shortens the life span and causes many other problems! One of my passions is helping people break the chains of poverty from a preventive health standpoint. We need to help educate our people on how to break out of poverty. It's the root cause of so many issues—psychological, social, economic, and medical. That's why I was so excited about this book. That's why empowering people on how to make multiple streams of income is so important! That's why I'm so excited about the field of real estate!

Why did you get into your industry?
My path into the field of real estate investing was a little unusual. Many people wonder why a physician would even be interested in this field. Let me explain. One of my major passions is preventive medicine, which is a field of medicine that involves looking at upstream factors and social determinants of health outcomes. Interestingly, one of the biggest social determinants of health outcomes is poverty and economic stability as I mentioned above. There were so many patients and families I would see come into the hospital with both minor and major medical conditions directly related to poverty. After a while, I got sick of not being able to do anything about it and having to deal with the *aftermath* of conditions related to poor living situations, lack of finances, lack of food resources, stress from financial struggles, and other burdens. Real estate was a way that I could learn to break the chains of poverty off my own generation line and eventually help teach others to do the same.

Real estate was also a way that I could have the freedom of time and could create a lasting legacy for my family. And most importantly, it was a potential way for me to create a passive stream of income, which was very important to me at the time I got started. At that time, I had just started my medical residency and was working up to 80 hours per week. I was so excited because I was finally living my dream of being a doctor, however, the amount of hours I was putting in to work each day was overwhelming. I was living my dream but was not able to see my family as much as I wanted to. I knew I could not live like that forever. I was not able to be there for certain events my kids had. I was living my dream, but it came at a cost. I knew then that I needed to find a way to transition my income over the long term to something passive so I could work my dream job only part time and free up other time to be with my family and pursue some of my other passions. I had been talking to others about real estate and reading books and attending seminars for years, but never found a way to get involved. But I knew then that it was time.

The final reason I got involved in real estate was because I was sick of my landlord taking all my money! We lived in a lovely duplex across the street from the hospital I trained at, but I got frustrated every year when he would conveniently increase the rent and happily collect his checks each month. He owned multiple properties on campus, and I was always amazed at that. I promised myself that one day I would be in his position. In my final year of medical school, he sent us a letter asking if we wanted to renew our lease, and my husband and I toiled with the decision. When I calculated how much money I had paid to him over the last 4 years of medical school I was shocked to discover it was almost $50,000! I thought to myself, I could have had a quarter of a house paid off by now! My husband finally gave me the push to stop being afraid of the unknown and jump into our destiny. My husband had been taking some property management classes on the side, and I had been talking with others involved in real estate and doing some research of my own. Although we did not have all the training in the world, we were ready to take the leap and enter into the world of real estate. It was scary, but we told our landlord we would not be renewing our lease and started the process of buying a duplex. That was one of the best choices I've made and was what propelled me into the field of real estate!

When it comes to being an entrepreneur, what do you love most about it?
Its very interesting how a lot of our young people are trained growing up—go to school, get good grades, get into college, then get a "good job" with a 401(K) working for someone else) so that you can retire by age sixty-five and have a nice life. Well, being an entrepreneur is so exciting because it breaks you out of this traditional mold!

Also, one of the things I absolutely love the most about being an entrepreneur is the ability to be creative. You see a vision, and then you are able to make it happen and execute it! The sky is the limit to what you can do! You are writing your own destiny, and *you* are in control. I love getting to make decisions, and I love the process of trial and error. For example, the house we currently live in is a duplex that we own and occupy, which means we live on one side and rent out the other side. Well, our old tenants had just moved out, and we needed to get the space ready for potential new tenants. My husband and I decided to make some updates to the space to be able to charge higher rent and make it more appealing. It was so fun and exciting getting to decide all the little details like exactly what updates to make, what color to paint the walls, which type of carpet to pick out, etc. I saw a vision in my mind of how I wanted the apartment to look, and I got to see it manifest. Based on our updates, we were then able to increase the rent by almost $300 per month! It was exciting to see how my decisions and my vision turned into profit.

What would you consider the pros about being in your industry?

There are many pros about being in the field of real estate investing. Personally, for me the top 4 are:

- The wide diversity of niches you can be involved in. Real estate is a huge field in which there are multiple different branches. There are many different avenues to make money in real estate. I love that because there are many different techniques and strategies and you can find which one best suits you to get started. For example, you can be involved in buy and holds, fix and flips, wholesaling, live-in flips, owner occupying (aka house hacking), real estate investment trusts, and so many more. The sky is the limit.
- When I first got started in real estate investing, I did not know there were low to no money down ways to get started. I thought you had to already be "rich" to get started, which is not the case. That is a pro!
- This is a market where there will *always* be demand. In 20-30 years, certain shoes or brands may go out of style, but a safe place to live will always be basic human need, so there will always be people looking to rent or buy homes.
- Real estate investing has the potential to create passive streams of income as I mentioned earlier. In certain areas of real estate like flipping or wholesaling, you are

working actively to make each check, however when you do buy and holds or other long term investments, they have the potential to create passive income. What this means is that you are making money while you sleep! You are also allowed the flexibility of time to spend with your family or to pursue other dreams.

Were you required to make any financial and/or time investments to get started?

The time investment that I made to first get started varied based on how busy I was each week. I started out with just doing a reading or two each night. I would talk with a person here or there each week, and I would listen to daily podcasts on the subject. When we were in the active phase of searching for homes, we were busier because we had to look at multiple properties, get prequalified for loans, complete a lot of paperwork, get inspections performed, etc. So there was definitely a time commitment, but it varied based on what else I had going on in my life at the time. That is the wonderful thing about real estate—you can go at whatever pace you want. You can walk, jog, or sprint to the finish line! You get out of it what you put in. Another major time commitment involved in getting into the field of real estate that no one really thinks about is the time commitment of saving money and getting your credit in order. For some, this can take years, but it is a very important step. The more money you have saved and the better your credit, the easier it will be to get started and the more options you will have regarding what field of real estate you want to get into. So putting in the time commitment to get those things in order is important. But remember, even if you don't have good credit or any money saved up, there are still ways to get involved in the field of real estate investing, and there are different strategies and techniques you can still use to make money. So don't let that hold you back.

Regarding the financial commitment to get started, it varies. Personally, when I first got started I was able to buy my duplex with no money down due to a special loan created for physicians. There are other loans of that type out there for veterans, military families, and other special situations. This opportunity was great for me because it helped boost me into the field of real estate. For those not able get a no-money-down loan, there are special loans that require only 3-5% down through the government if you owner-occupy the home (live in one of the units yourself). These can be used not only for single family homes, but duplexes, triplexes and fourplexes as well. If you were to try to buy a duplex, triplex or fourplex for the purpose of simply renting all of the units out without living there personally then the down payment is more like 25-30 percent on average! That is why using the owner occupant route to get into the field of real estate is so amazing! You get into the house for a low down payment, and then in a few years you can move out and then rent out *all* the units. By doing it that way, you avoid paying the large down payment up front. You can repeat this process over and over as you build your real estate empire. This technique is so awesome because you learn the ropes of being a landlord and have someone else pay your mortgage while you save up for your next big move/purchase. I highly encourage anyone interested in real estate investing to make their next goal to purchase a multifamily unit to owner occupy. Instead of aspiring to purchase a single family "dream home," change your mindset and purchase a multifamily unit to live in and rent out! It is a shift in thinking, but I believe a multifamily residential unit (1-4 units) should be everyone's first home purchase! This is by far one of the best ways to get involved in real estate investing!

What are the statistics of success in your industry?
According to a survey of U.S. millionaires by Morgan Stanley, 77 percent of individuals with $1 million or more in assets invested in real estate in 2014.

Also, according to the American Academy of Pediatrics, childhood poverty is a significant determinant of health. It affects not only physical and developmental health, but also educational achievement, emotional well-being, and health into adulthood. Poverty is defined as a family income of $24,000 or less per year for a family of four. Kids who live in poverty are at higher risks for teen pregnancy, drug and alcohol abuse, high school dropout, criminal behavior, and exposure to "toxic stress," which can have lasting physiologic and emotional effects into adulthood.

What is the average income in your industry?
Again, the income in the field of real estate investing varies widely. It all depends on your particular niche and how involved you are. It also varies based on your region. You can make negative income to upwards of millions of dollars in this field! I know people who make as low as $20,000 per year to greater than $200,000 per year so it really varies based on how large your portfolios are, your technique for investing, and much more. That is why the world of real estate investing is so exciting! You get out what you put in. Most people choose a certain amount of monthly income they desire and then do whatever it takes to acquire that amount. Everyone has different personal goals regarding how much money they want to make in real estate. You pick a number and then figure out what you have to do to make it happen! For example, if you want to be able to quit your nine-to-five job, you'd need to determine how much money your family needs on a monthly basis to survive. If you net $3,000 per month on your job, you'd need to figure out a way to make $3,000 monthly through various strategies in real estate to replace that income, whether it be fix and flips, buy and holds, wholesaling, etc. Let's say you obtain a rental property where you make $750 in net profit each month. If you could, over time, obtain four of those, you would be bringing in $3,000 per month and could essentially quit your nine-to-five. Although you would have to maintain the properties from time to time, *you* would get to decide when to put in the hours. *You* would be your own boss. What would you do with all that extra time? You could use it to pursue other ways to create multiple streams of income, you could travel, or spend time with loved ones. Remember that your time is as valuable if not more valuable than money. I view the *time* that will be freed up in the future for me as a result of my real estate investments as the true measure of income!

So basically to answer the original question, the average income varies but mostly depends on the amount you choose you want to make and how serious you are about the actions you need to take to achieve it! Also "income" in the field of real estate can be measured in the forms of both money and time. It depends on how you look at it.

When it comes to success in your industry, what are 3 main tips you would give to those interested in doing what you do?

- Be careful who you trust with your money.
- Have a plan of action and stick to it.
- Be persistent and never give up on your dreams! Don't let roadblocks stop you from pursuing your dream, just figure out a better way to get around them.

When actively working in your industry, what does a day (week) look like for you?

Each day varies. For me, I have been blessed to have tenants that do not often have complaints or questions, so for the most part, the month is quiet. I have also learned that automating things is very helpful, especially the process of rent collection. When we first started, my husband and I would personally collect the rent checks. We would then take them to the bank every month and cash them. Now, we use an online rent payment system which is great and saves a lot of time. I also do a lot of email and electronic communication with my tenants as well. I'm also in the process of learning to utilize virtual assistants to help with some of my future property acquisitions and other deals. My weeks are busier during times of tenant turnover or when repairs are needed. But this can be overcome with a property manager or hiring out the work. As I mentioned, I try to delegate as many things as possible.

Do you have a mentor?

I have had several wonderful mentors on my road to starting out in real estate. One of my biggest tips is to be bold and reach out to connect with people who are where you would like to be in ten years. One of my first mentors was a successful female minority real estate investor from my area. I was introduced to her through a friend from church who knew I was interested in real estate investing. I started by hearing her story of how and why she got into real estate, and she really spent a lot of time explaining to me the ins and outs of the business. She is primarily into buy and holds, which was something I was interested in at the time. She sent me copies of her leases and other documentation for me to see examples. She talked me through her process of selecting tenants and taught me the importance of providing quality rentals. One of the biggest lessons I learned from her is that the quality of your rental attracts the right tenants. Never let greed cause you to cut corners and become a "slum landlord." She also taught me to be confident in myself and to always remain professional. She talked to me about how she experienced racism at times in this field, and people often did not expect her to be the landlord/homeowner. She taught me how she did not let this get her down but instead used this to make her business and drive for success stronger. It was amazing working with her.

I also had the pleasure of learning about wholesaling and finding homes for purchase that are not listed on the MLS through a mentor from my hometown in Milwaukee. I saw his ads and his company online and reached out. I asked if I could partner with him and assist him with some deals, which would be of mutual benefit because I would be able to learn the ropes as well. This was a wonderful experience, and I learned a lot working with him. The main lesson he taught me was about the art of negotiation. When negotiating, even if you ask for a low price that seems ridiculous, you must ask with confidence! I learned a lot from him and still work with him on deals occasionally even today. Mentors are great because they have the potential to turn into business partners you can do deals with in the future.

Other indirect mentors into the field of real estate have been my parents. They owner occupied duplexes as we were growing up, and this heightened a thirst within me to become an entrepreneur myself. I truly thank them for this! They still give me encouragement even today and help support me with all of my dreams.

I have had several other wonderful mentors along the way I am truly grateful for. My main piece of advice to anyone interested in getting started in real estate is to maximize the amount of free information you can get before spending thousands and thousands of dollars on training programs with "gurus" who claim they can teach you the secret to success. It is okay to spend a couple hundred dollars on books and introductory trainings/coaching sessions, but spending thousands and thousands of dollars just for your education is not necessary. You would be surprised with the amount of knowledge you can get by simply asking people who are in the field how they got started and if they have any tips for those new to real estate. If you make the goal to email or call one new person in the field of real estate investing each week to connect and introduce yourself, you will have a host of mentors and possible future business partners! I keep a list of all my contacts and potential mentors in the field. I write down a brief paragraph about who they are, what they do, and possible ways we can connect in the future. This has been a great strategy for me. For the most part, people are happy to help out. There are also many mentors on online sites and real estate social networks. My favorite site of all time is www.biggerpockets.com. I learned so much from that site, connected with so many great people, and I would recommend it to anyone looking to get started in real estate.

Has being in your industry helped you to expand to other industries?
Yes! Being involved in real estate has opened up so many doors. My strategy of owner occupying as a means to get started in real estate was very helpful because the money I received covered my entire mortgage payments plus some. I was then able to save the money I would have been spending on the mortgage for other ventures and future real estate purchases. Being involved in real estate also heightened my passion for helping others use real estate as a tool for economic freedom and last year I was able to team up with 4 other young entrepreneurs interested in real estate to start a company where we pool our money to pursue further investments. We are also in the process of planning outreach and educational programs to help others get started in this field who traditionally would not have been able to in the past. I have also been able to use the experience of being an entrepreneur to talk with kids in a variety of settings about reaching their dreams and becoming their own boss. That has,

by far, been one of the most rewarding things that has come out of this. I love teaching kids the difference between renting and owning and how they have the potential to change the trajectory of their lives through real estate investing. I have done sessions fun, interactive sessions middle schoolers dealing with money and real estate. I do simulations where they get to decide which type of house to buy and how much rent to charge. We calculate what their net profit would be and go through different scenarios. I love seeing their eyes light up when they add up all the numbers! I love inspiring kids to be entrepreneurs, and being an entrepreneur myself has allowed me to reach out to them.

The funds from real estate investing have also allowed me to get my feet wet in other industries like E-commerce and online sales. It has also opened up doorways for me to become and author and pursue my dreams of public speaking.

Finally, being involved in real estate further heightened my interest in helping others achieve economic freedom and personal finance success. This because I noticed many people I talked with who were interested in home ownership or investing were not able to due to poor credit or lack of funds. I especially noticed this in certain minority populations, and especially in women of color. For this reason and others, I teamed up with a group of wonderful women to form a social network called Brown Girl Green Money—women of color working together to reach financial freedom and support each other along the way. We started out planning to simply do a blog on personal finance but were blessed to get a weekly column in a local newspaper. Now the column runs in newspapers in two different cities! We talk about a variety of topics, and home ownership and real estate investing is one of them. We have now partnered with a local bank to host live money meet up/support groups for women interested in achieving economic freedom and being strengthened in the area of personal finance. We will be inviting in guest speakers on lots of different topics, and positioning yourself financially for home ownership and real estate investing will definitely be one of them. I'm so excited about this! We are actively looking to expand our group to different cities. We are in the process of turning it into a non-profit organization, so I'm excited about that as well.

So yes, this field has opened up many doors and I'm excited about the many doors it will open up in the future!

If someone was to come to you for help what would be the first thing you would tell them in regards to getting started in your industry?
To get started I'd say take these 6 easy steps:

1. Start with signing up for an account on www.biggerpockets.com. This was the website that changed my life. They have educational materials, podcasts, articles, mentorship, and purchasing opportunities. This site will give you a great overview of the field of real estate investing and will also help you choose what particular niche/strategy you want to get started with. On the site, download the free book, *Bigger Pockets Presents: The Ultimate Beginner's Guide to Real Estate Investing* by Joshua Dorkin and Brandon Turner. Read 1-2 chapters each day.
2. After reading that book and browsing the site, pick a niche in real estate investing that you want to get started in. For example, wholesaling, fix and flipping, buy and hold, notes, vacation properties, etc. Picking the way you will get started in real estate investing will depend on a lot of factors, including how much money you have saved up, if you want to do it full or part time, if you have someone to partner with, your time commitment, where you live and how much risk you want to take. The great thing is there is something for everyone!
3. Read and learn as much as you can about the field/strategy you finally do choose. Take 30-60 minutes each day to read an article or watch a video/podcast related to that field.
4. Contact one person per week who is successful in the field of your choice. Call email them and simply ask to chat by phone about how they got involved in real

estate and to learn more about their business. Keep a log of everyone you talk to, because you may be able to reach out to them in the future. As you talk to different people, you will identify which ones are good fits for you and which ones can be potential mentors in the future. Also, don't forget when taking this step to be bold! Currently, I live across the street from a multimillion dollar apartment complex. I often drive by, reach out my hand and say, "I will own that one day!" One night, I got bold and looked up the owner of the complex. I discovered he was a rich man who owned multiple properties across the state and was a multimillionaire! I didn't let this hold me back, and I decided to call his office to request a meeting with him! The worse that could happen is that the receptionist would laugh at me and hang up, but the best that could happen is that I would get a meeting. They were a little confused at first as to why I was calling, but in the end and with some persistence, I was able to get the meeting approved. I'm still in the process of scheduling an actual date to meet with him, but just the fact that I even have the opportunity is amazing! So all that to say, be bold when selecting mentors and don't limit yourself.

5. Create a six-month plan of action and set weekly and monthly goals on how you will achieve that goal. Write the goals down somewhere you can see them every day and speak positive affirmations each day. Life and death is in the power of the tongue! Also, if you have the time consider picking up a part time job in a real estate *related* field to gain more knowledge while you are getting prepared to make your first personal investment (ex: leasing agent, property manager, real estate agent, handyman, receptionist at an existing real estate firm, etc). Also over the next few months make sure to attend your local Real Estate Investment Association (REIA) meetings. They are in every major city and usually the first couple visits are free. Use that as a place to network and get to know people already successful in the field.

6. And finally, just jump in! You must avoid what we call in the world of real estate, "analysis paralysis." What this means is reading and learning so much about so many different topics that you get overwhelmed and end up taking no action because you are paralyzed with the vast amount of information out there and fear of failure. Let me ask you a question: when you learned to ride a bike, did you read a book about it first or spend years and years studying and analyzing it? No, you learned by just jumping on it and seeing what happened! This is how I look at getting started in real estate. It is important to gain a base of knowledge, but then you have to just take action and jump in. You will learn by trial and error. As situations arise, you will have to seek help for the answers, and you will learn so much along the way. I have learned so much more by actually getting my hands dirty and being confronted with situations I have to figure out how to handle than by all the books and readings and trainings I did. You have to be brave, take risks, and then just jump in!

Outside of working (in your industry) what is your favorite thing to do?

I love spending time with my family! Family is so very important to me. My younger brother, Aaron, passed away suddenly at age 16 while I was in college. We were best friends, and many people thought we were twins! One Saturday morning when I was on my college campus, I got a call telling me they could not wake him up. I rushed over to the house, and as I was running in I saw the paramedics walking out without him! I ran into the house, and to my horror my parents told me that they could not revive him and that he had passed away. This changed my life forever and I am still healing from this devastating loss, but what it taught me is that tomorrow is not promised, and that you have to cherish each day that you have. You might be laughing and joking with a loved one today and they will be gone tomorrow. So family is so very, very, very important to me, and I love spending time with family and friends. Life is too short, and I love doing anything with people that make me laugh and just enjoy life! In particular, I love playing monopoly and going to trampoline parks with my kids. My favorite time of the day is seeing them after work and them running up to me giving me a big hug. My favorite thing to do is anything that makes them smile. I love long talks and laughs with my mom as we figure out how to "make life work"! I love going out to eat with friends and laughing so hard the waitresses have to ask us to quiet down. My favorite thing to eat is king crab legs. My favorite day of the week is Tuesday because it's date night with my husband! I also love playing volleyball and singing. I lead a community choir in town spreading the message of hope, strength and the power to overcome, and that is also one of the biggest joys in my life. I *love* inspiring kids to reach for the stars and teaching them that they can be anything they set their minds to. When I am doing those favorite things, I am happy!

Do you provide coaching or resources to anyone who wants to further educate themselves in your industry?
Yes! I do not personally provide long term coaching in real estate investing, but I do offer one time motivational and empowerment introductory coaching sessions to those who are interested in getting started. I help them determine which niche is best for them, give them motivation and encouragement, and then point them in the right direction with resources and specific tips on how to continue along their journey. It's kind of like a jump starter package. I am planning to extend these services further through the work I do with the new real estate investing company I started with the other young investors I mentioned above and through Brown Girl Green Money. I also do motivational speaking and workshops for kids interested in becoming entrepreneurs and give talks on the connection between health and poverty. I am very excited for what the future holds!

Is there anything you don't necessarily love about the industry?
The biggest downside of real estate investing for me personally is the fear of the unknown. If you purchase a property or rent out to a certain tenant, you don't know what will happen in the future. The furnace might randomly break or the tenant may randomly decide not to pay their rent, so sometimes it's hard.

But as I mentioned earlier, all of the potential downsides can be overcome with planning and proper screening.

What favorite marketing strategies have you used to help with building your business?
My favorite three marketing strategies have involved using Craigslist ads, word of mouth, and referrals. The biggest one I would emphasize is talking with people in person or on the phone. This has worked the best for me! Developing relationships is key!

What are 3 books that you recommend for success in your industry?

- *The Book on Investing in Real Estate with No (and Low) Money Down: Real Life Strategies for Investing in Real Estate Using Other People's Money* - Brandon Turner
- *Rich Dad Poor Dad: What The Rich Teach Their Kids About Money That the Poor and Middle Class Do Not!* - Robert T. Kiyosaki
- *BiggerPockets Presents: The Ultimate Beginner's Guide to Real Estate Investing* - Joshua Dorkin and Brandon Turner

If there was one thing you may have done differently in your industry when you got started, what would it have been?
I would have started out even earlier in my real estate investing journey. I bought my first property three years ago at age 26. If I could do it over again, I would have bought a fourplex in college and lived in one unit while I rented out the other three units to fellow college members! I would have also gotten involved in more low and no money down strategies for real estate investing that I have learned over the years at a younger age.

What is your favorite quote?
"Never give up on your dreams" —Rev. Dr. Sandy L. Johnson, Jr.

Special thanks to the following:

Ronald Burford
Owner - Burford Promotions RRE
Facebook.com/BurfordPromotions

Julie O'Clary
Executive Consultant - Rodan + Fields
Facebook.com/Julie.OClary

Mack Daniels Jr
Car Salesman/Travel Agent - Dream Trips
Facebook.com/mad24dreamtrips

Ricky Franklin and Naomi Khalil
Owners/Administrators - Arise Personal Care Care Services
Facebook.com/AriseCare

Lawrence N Adams III
Founding Member - Wayaka Perfection
Facebook.com/wakayaperfectionplus

Julia Grace Saffold
Entrepreneur, Inspirational Speaker, Choral Director - New
Season Shift
Facebook.com/newseasonshift

Tia Murray, BS
Labor & Postpartum Doula, Childbirth Educator, Sociologist -
Birth Wise Doula Services
Facebook.com/BirthWiseWithADoula

Victoria Banks
Brand Consultant, Independent Representative - AVON
Facebook.com/VictoriaBanksBeauty

Venus Washington
Empowerment Coach, Fitness Instructor, Owner - RU FIT
Facebook.com/rufit6

Bonita Nunez
Real Estate Agent - Keller Williams
Facebook.com/bonita.nunez.50

Wayne and Aquilla Battle
Manager/Registered Nurse Entrepreneur

LeaDrean N. Jordan
Drill Sergeant (Staff Sergeant) - United States Army

James Bell, CLTC
Financial Advisor and Field Director

Urban Sol Inc.
Jessica Jeremiah MSW, LCSW
Richard and Dionne Tinch
Vanessa Young
Tonya Roginski and Tammy Franda
Orpha Battle, RN
Milton and Jennifer Hines

Tiffany Moneak-Howard

Industry - Beauty Industry
Instagram.com/SalonMoneak
Facebook.com/TiffanyMoneak
Twitter.com/SalonMoneak
Linkedin.com/in/tiffanymoneak
www.SalonMoneak.com

Master hairstylist, entrepreneur, and beauty mogul in the making with more than twelve years of experience in the haircare industry.

Graduated from Charles Academy of Beauty in Mobile, Alabama, and became a licensed master cosmetologist.

Later in her career, Tiffany went on to train under the direction and mentorship of celebrity stylist and beauty expert, Sherita Cherry, the owner Sherita Cherry University and Genesis Hair Art in Atlanta, GA.

As a committed beauty professional and entrepreneur, Tiffany's passion and consistency for education has played a major role in the success of her career. Today Tiffany is the owner/operator at Salon Moneak and Salon Moneak Pop-up, a VIP mobile salon.

In addition to managing her busy schedule of being a mom, wife, and BOSS (Business Owner Serving and Succeeding) Tiffany finds time to serve in her community. She is an active member of BWN (Black Women Networking) International.

How long have you been in your industry?
For as long as I remember I have been fascinated with hair! After graduating high school in 2000, I attended Charles Academy of Beauty in Mobile, Alabama. I began my career working as an assistant (Do not despise small beginnings!). After graduating from beauty school and obtaining my cosmetology license in 2003, I moved to Atlanta to continue on my successful journey in the beauty industry.

Why did you get into your industry?
I realized that I had a passion for styling hair at an early age. As a child, my mother would take me to the beauty salon to have my hair styled. I loved to sit and watch all the hairstylists in the salon deliver their creativity as they styled each client's hair. I remember feeling a sense of joy from the salon atmosphere each time that I entered. The energy from the stylist and the music in the salon were an added bonus for me.

When it comes to being an entrepreneur, what do you love most about it?

Being an entrepreneur has given me the freedom and ability to set my own schedule. I'm in control of my own time, and not bound by a traditional nine-to-five job. I hate tradition, by the way. I love the fact that I can have flexibility, which is very much needed to be able to balance being a wife and mother of four.

What would you say are the pros to being an entrepreneur?

There are many pros to being a hairstylist. One of the biggest pros for me is being able to serve others while making them feel beautiful and confident. As a hairstylist, you come in contact with lots of different people every day with different professions and personalities, and you have to be able to readjust with each client that you are providing a service for, which can be very challenging at times, but in the end can be very rewarding. This just helps to keep you on your toes and increases your confidence in your work. It also gives me an outlet for my creativity. The most rewarding thing about my industry is that I get to make money doing something that I love.

Were you required to make any financial and/or time investments to get started?

My initial investment was $1,000 for a small 700 sq. ft. studio space. For contracting and salon equipment, I invested somewhere around $2,000. I have always been a firm believer that in order to make money you have to spend money. One *big* mistake often made by entrepreneurs is that we will spend countless hours and countless dollars on things like marketing and advertising when the reality is that we don't have a clear direction as to what our brand is, who our target market is going to be, or what the ultimate goal for your business really is. In other words, until you have sat done and written out your blueprint, set your goals, and created a strategy, or as I call it, a "game plan," you should not spend a lot of money on marketing and advertising. Instead, invest in the person behind the brand. Invest in yourself through continued education and finding mentorship. Finding someone who has been where you are going, someone who has made mistakes, fallen down, got back up, and has gained success that you desire to have is going to be a major key to the success of your business.

What are the statistics of success in your industry?
The hair-care industry is now one of the fastest growing industries in the U.S., with more than 900,000 total establishments and annual sales of nearly $40 billion.

What is the average income in your industry?
On average hairstylist bring home about $45,000 a year. However, the great thing about being a master cosmetologist/salon owner is that you have the ability to control how much money you make a year by using your platform as a beauty industry professional to create additional streams of income.

When it comes to success in your industry, what are main tips you would give to those interested in doing what you do?
There are several factors that play a major role in the success of your hair-care business.

- Find Your Niche. What is it that you are passionate about? As beauty professionals, we often times try to be all things to all people. I would consider myself a "jack of all trades" when it comes to my industry. However, I've also realized throughout the course of my career that being able to identify your niche or your target market is very important. It paints a clear picture of who you are, what it is that you offer, and who you want to offer it too.
1. Set Goals and Plan. As a hairstylist, you should consistently set goals and plan out how you are going to achieve those goals. Be consistent! For example, if your goal is to earn $100,000, it's as simple as finding 100 clients that will pay you $1,000 a year. How are you going to find those 100 clients?
2. Use What You Have. Hairstylists often times get caught up in trying to always market to new clients that we forget to start with what we already have. The best form

116

of advertisement is word of mouth. Get referrals! Having a referral program is one of the most powerful marketing strategies a hairstylist can use. How do you get your clients to send referrals? *Simply ask!* It is a vulnerable, terrifying thing to do as a stylist, but believe it or not, clients *like* to help. The perfect time to ask a client for referrals is before they leave the chair. Once you see that the client is pleased with their service and while they are admiring their hair in the mirror is the time to jump in with your referral pitch! Here is an example of one that I use:

> "Thanks for coming in today Jane! It was a pleasure doing your hair and getting to know you. I'm glad you like your hair. I would love to see more clients like you. If you know anyone who's in need of a new cut or color, send them my way. I'll be sure to thank you with a 25 percent discount off your next service."

3. Be sure to offer an incentive that is worth their while. Clients love to see the WIIFM (what's in it for me). Think of the bigger picture when creating your incentive. What is your current client worth? Clients who consistently bring in referrals should be awarded accordingly.

4. Implementing a loyalty program is also a very important marketing strategy in Using what you have. While searching for new clients, hairstylists often overlook their loyal clients, but remember that every paying client is valuable and should be rewarded for their loyalty. For example, you can offer them a free service after a certain number of visits, or when a client spends a certain dollar amount on retail products in your salon, you may want to offer them a free product or a gift certificate to use towards products or services. The goal is to keep them coming back and to keep them bragging to others about you, your product or service.

5. Keep Track Of What Works - Choosing a great software program for your salon business is essential in keeping track of referrals and loyal clients, and it also helps keep track of inventory and profit/loss. Here of some of the most trending programs out today: Bizlinkms.com, Vigaro, StyleSeat, and Shedulicity to name a few. Choose what works best for you!

When actively working in your industry, what does a day (week) look like for you?

My goal is to be able to run a successful business while maintaining a healthy balanced, abundant life that God has created for me to have. I am learning that consistency is one major key to my success as well as staying in the "state of flow." I am a wife and a mother of four, so I am a firm believer that in order to be successful at anything, and in order to walk in the exceedingly abundant life that God has created for us, we must keep a balance, and for me, that has been keeping God first, family, then business. A day in the life of Tiffany-Moneak starts at about 5:30 a.m. with what I call my "daily success routine." I start off every morning with prayer and meditation. I do some type of quick ten-to-fifteen-minute workout to get my creative juices flowing. I get the kids fed and off to school. I prioritize my daily tasks according to what I have planned on my calendar. My goal as a hairstylist is to be able to build relationships and collaborate with other beauty industry professionals who are serious and passionate about this industry. I want to reach out to at least ten to twenty industry professionals per month. I set a goal to attend at least two networking events a month, produce one hair/fashion show a year, and host one beauty workshop tour per year.

Do you have a mentor?

Absolutely! I truly believe that having a mentor is a very important key to your success. For me I have several mentors, but all for different areas of my life. There's my spiritual mentor who encourages me and prays with me through my everyday life changes whether it be with family, business, or my faith walk.

I have a business mentor who is a very dear friend of mine and also an industry professional who has had great success.

I also have two business coaches. One is business resource and stand out coach, Taurea Avant, who has inspired and helped me to be able to write a book in thirty days, book speaking gigs, and she has taught me how to get the most out of social media marketing. Then I have my beauty industry coach who teaches me different strategies on how to achieve success as a leader in the beauty industry, and she holds me accountable. They all have taught me how to use my creativity to stand out in this crowded world.

Has being in your industry helped you to expand to other industries?
Being in the beauty industry has definitely led to other businesses for me. I am currently in the process of starting my own wigs and hair extensions line and a traveling beauty agency.

If someone was to come to you for help what would be the first thing you would tell them in regards to getting started in your industry?
Always keep God first! Invest in yourself, find a mentor, and always remain teachable.

Outside of working (in your industry) what is your favorite thing to do?
Outside of working in my industry and spending time with my family, I love to get in the presence of God. I am a true worshiper at heart, and so for me this is what brings me peace, joy, love, balance, and focus, and it puts me in a state of flow so I am able to have a clear direction of the path that God has for me. I also enjoy singing, dancing, and spending time with family.

Do you provide coaching or resources to anyone who wants to further educate themselves in your industry?
I am currently working on putting together a mentorship program to help other stylists stand out and become experts in the beauty industry.

Is there anything you don't necessarily love about the industry?
The one thing that I dislike about some people in my industry is we have made this industry become a competition, and so we sometimes want to keep everything to ourselves instead of creating an opportunity to collaborate with others and share knowledge on how to build successful brands for our industry.

What favorite marketing strategies have you used to help with building your business?
Online marketing systems such as bizlink, mindbody, and styleseat are all personal favorites of mine. Each of these software programs allow you to market your salon efficiently and affordably by keeping track of client services info. They allow you to send out appointment reminders to clients, thus cutting down on no call no shows. I love the fact that I can customize the program to send out a friendly message to my clients when it is time to come in for their next cut, color, or other chemical service. This helps to increase client retention.

What are 3 books that you recommend for success in your industry?

1. *Balance, Focus, and The Flow* - Tiffany Moneak-Howard
2. *Assisting Rules!: The Ultimate Guide to Assisting Makeup Artists and Hairstylists in Beauty, Fashion, and Print* - DeShawn Hatcher
3. *It's Not Really About the Hair: The Honest Truth about Life, Love, and the Business of Beauty* - Tabatha Coffey

If there was one thing you may have done differently in your industry when you got started, what would it have been?
I absolutely love working in my industry. The only regret that I have is not investing in hiring a coach earlier on in my career. Having a coach has helped grow my hair care business tremendously! Since hiring a coach, I have been able to learn how to put my focus in the right place and not be all over the

place spending countless dollars and valuable time on non-effective marketing.

What is your favorite quote?
"For I know the thoughts that I think towards you saith the Lord, thoughts of peace, and not of evil, to give you an expected end." Jeremiah 29:11 King James Version

Special Thanks to the following Pre-Order Supporters

Candace Holyfield Randle
Business Owner
I Love Candy Spa Parties and Massage
Facebook.com/candace.h.randle

Beverly Campbell
Business Owner at Office Ink
Facebook.com/beverly.campbell.7

Melynda Powers
Independent Rep and Brand Partner at
Silpada Designs and Nerium International
Facebook.com/melynda.shelton

Lashunda Gibby
Workforce Administrator
ATT

Nisha Rocker
Clerk PSE
USPS
Facebook.com/valaneciarocmc

Lakeshia Dixon
Store Manager
Walgreens
Facebook.com/lakeshia.dixon

Jerilyn Pugh
Clinical Assistant/Medical assistant optometry

Premier Medical
Facebook.com/jerilyn.pugh

Deardra Frowner
Business Owner/Entreprenuer at
LavishLyfe Inc.
Facebook.com/mrzdee.west

Dannella Burnett

Industry - Event Planning
Instagram.com/DannellaBurnett
Facebook.com/OakwoodOccasions
Periscop.tv/DannellaBurnett
Twitter.com/OakwoodOccasion
Linkedin.com/in/DannellaBurnett
www.OakwoodOccasions.com

With a love of food and Julia Child as her inspiration, Dannella Burnett has worked in the field of culinary and special events since the age of 16. She holds degrees in culinary arts and food service management from Johnson & Wales University. Among other awards, Dannella has earned gold medals in international culinary competitions in the U.K. and Germany.

Following college, she managed restaurants, catered and coordinated events and weddings in Washington, D.C., and Virginia. In 2009, when her husband lost his job in the construction field, Dannella created Oakwood Occasions to provide North Georgia with quality event solutions and to support her family.

"Necessity may be the mother of invention, but mothers are inventive by necessity," quotes Dannella. Over the last seven years, Oakwood Occasions has offered custom catering, high end vending options, OO fudge shipped nationally, coffee services with Organo Coffee, OO Coffee Shoppe, OO Café and event management and wedding coordination. In 2015, Oakwood Occasions streamlined operations and now offers event solutions and production, wedding planning, and coordination in addition to operating the OO Café in the Hall County Government Center featuring Organo Coffees and Teas.

Dannella has been featured in several publications. She has been named in Gwinnett Magazine's People to Know for two years in a row, and was recently named North Georgia's best event planner and was recognized for best wedding cakes. She has become an author and sought-after speaker for women's empowerment and small business ownership and event solutions. Dannella is truly a creative entrepreneur who believes in multiple streams of income and always finding the win-win-win combination. Through creative partnerships with her incredible network as well as high level of experience, Dannella brings everything to the table needed to make your event a success!

How long have you been in your industry?

My parents were very encouraging when I surprised them with my desire to be a chef at the early age of nine after seeing Julia Child on TV. Julia's love of food was infectious. I was immediately drawn in. My parents were further surprised that the desire to become a chef remained in me. They were subjected to all my early culinary attempts including treats such as Death by Chocolate after a full Thanksgiving feast and soufflés with more batter on the ceiling than in the pan! I entered the industry at age fifteen with my first mentor, Lenore Emery, catering alongside her students from an advanced program at a local school. That was more than thirty years ago!

Why did you get into your industry?

I really was hooked from the get go. The passion I saw in Julia Child first inspired me to play in the kitchen drove me to assist at the special events and weddings with Lenore Emory. I love being a part of the significant memories in people's lives. When it was time to look at universities, my only desire was to study culinary arts at Johnson & Wales University in Rhode Island. Every step of the way, every new experience, has kept me engaged and furthered my desire and passion for events. I had the opportunity in school to audition and secure a spot for the first US student culinary team where I trained under Master Chef Noel Cullen. After training, our team accompanied Chef Cullen to Hotel Olympia in London and Ika Hoga in Frankfurt, West Germany. As individual competing chefs, and as a team, we brought home gold medals from both international competitions.

When it comes to being an entrepreneur, what do you love most about it?

I love the diversity, the need for self-motivation, and the limitless possibilities. As an entrepreneur, I can participate in creative partnerships and create my own systems. Each day has new opportunities, new interactions, and potential. I love that the responsibility and rewards are equally in my hands. I have areas of my business that are strictly my company as well as areas where I have partnered with other companies or other entrepreneurs. Those kinds of partnerships are not typically available working for others. I love the flexibility in the job. Of course you have to be prepared for some long hours. You've probably heard the saying, "Entrepreneurs only work half days, the first 12 hours or the second 12 hours!" Some days are even longer than that, but it is always a choice, and if I choose to take a family day or vacation or put my nose to the grindstone, it is my choice and my responsibility. I think all successful entrepreneurs have found the way to thrive on finding the balance of risk versus. reward and love the adrenaline rush of new possibilities.

What would you consider the pros about being in your industry?

In the event and special occasions industry, I think I'm truly blessed to be a part of creating professional and personal visions that make up the memories of companies and individuals as well as creating the platforms that allow others to shine. I love the whole creative process of discovering my clients' vision, bringing together the elements, seeing the event take shape, and that moment in an event where *everything* clicks. A lot of my professional clients, which include medium to large corporations, non-profits, business and networking associations and venues, are dreamers, big picture people who need a detailed, logistical partner to adapt or guide their vision, share their message, or accomplish their goal. My brides and personal event clients have a vision close to their heart. It's quite the honor and privilege to facilitate those memories that last a lifetime.

Were you required to make any financial and/or time investments to get started?

We started Oakwood Occasions after my husband was laid off when the recession hit the construction/building industry so hard in Atlanta in 2008. We didn't know immediately what we would do with two little ones at home. A woman at my church actually suggested we explore using our church kitchen, which is what we did. With no budget and no business plan, we launched Oakwood Occasions. We went to networking groups and used Facebook and word of mouth to grow. Probably one-half of all income went back into the business for equipment and tools, but we began to grow. As we put food on others' tables, we put food on our own. I'm a believer that "necessity is the mother of invention, but mothers are inventive by necessity!" Eventually the business grew to the point where we invested in a website, accounting software, vehicles, more equipment, china, linens, décor, tents, tables, marketing materials, and so much more. In fact, for Mother's Day in 2013, instead of flowers and a brunch out with family, we picked up a 10 foot box truck with a lift gate as a new investment in the company! Time has always been a big investment for this industry, but the hard work has paid off. In the beginning, it certainly felt like I worked 24/7; however, we're now at a point where I can pick and choose some of my daily activities and have a bit more balance in my schedule.

What are the statistics of success in your industry?
According to the Department of Labor, in 2014 there were over 100,000 jobs in meetings, conventions, and events. The industry is expected to grow by over 10% over the next decade and grow faster than the national average. While education may not be required, it is projected that the best possibilities exist for those with bachelor's degrees in meeting and event management, hospitality or tourism management.

What is the average income in your industry?
The average income, again according to the Department of Labor, is $46,490. The pay for specialists or entrepreneurs in the industry is higher at $63,880.

When it comes to success in your industry, what are 3 main tips you would give to those interested in doing what you do?

1. **Understand the big picture so you can tend to the smallest details.** Really listen to and talk with your client. You need to see the broader scope so you can fill in the elements needed for a successful event and stay true to a budget, a vision, and a purpose. My professional clients have an agenda and a goal, my brides have a vision. It is my job to keep them on that

path so the end result is in line and accomplishes those objectives. You need to understand budgets, how to work with other professionals, industry standards, and the mechanics of particular event models.

2. **Check your Motives.** You must have a strong desire to make another's vision yours within your own vision. You need to have the passion for you and your client. There will be setbacks, changes, compromises, and challenges. You need to maintain focus and drive to overcome challenges for your own goals, but more importantly for each individual client.

3. **Stay a Student.** This industry is ever-changing. New technologies, new modalities, new marketing, and new concepts are constantly being added into the event planning mix. I've always adopted an attitude of, "yes we can, even if we have to figure out how!" Be open to new ways of accomplishing tasks for yourself and your clients that include new software and new ideas while retaining your signature expertise.

When actively working in your industry, what does a day (week) look like for you?

I don't think any day mirrors another. With the diversity within our companies I may have any or all of the following activities: attending networking events, emails, phone calls to clients or vendors, venue site visits, client meetings, shopping for new elements, securing rentals, placing orders, conference calls with clients or business partners, dream building, reading new materials, training, gathering, scheduling, paying bills, stressing about paying bills, invoicing clients, accounting, writing contracts, having coffee or one-on-ones with other business owners, clients or prospects, interviewing new interns or employees, meeting with my accountant, lawyers or other professionals, coaching sessions for personal and professional development, setting up and executing events, brainstorming, marketing on Facebook, LinkedIn, Twitter, Pinterest, Instagram, or Periscope, or learning about the newest form of social media, following others in my field or related fields in those social media platforms, creating graphics or ordering graphics and signage for events. The list is endless, which is why organization and setting priorities are critical. In the midst of all of this, you must also care for yourself, your family and your mental well-being!

Do you have a mentor?

Over the years I've had many coaches and mentors, some for short periods of time to learn very specific lessons and some over many years and changes. My first mentor, Lenore Emery, was the teacher who took me under her wing and taught me alongside her students to cater, serve, and plan caterings and events. She was a friend of the family and instilled a great work ethic and great love of service to others in me. It's because of Lenore's encouragement and example that I went on to culinary school and have some of the core knowledge I still use today.

In college I was selected as one of six students to train under Master Chef Noel Cullen from Ireland and prepared to compete in two international culinary competitions. We attended and competed in Hotel Olympia in London, England and Ika Hoga in Frankfurt, West Germany. Chef Cullen taught me that you must be prepared "like soldiers in battle." There may be little time for rational thought and weighing of options when the moment comes, and pure instinct and training must override fear, adrenaline, and the challenge ahead of you. I'm so grateful for the experiences with this incredible teacher and the other students from Johnson & Wales. At one point we were the only students from the U.S. that had competed in these prestigious competitions, where three of us earned gold medals from both events.

Over the next several years in Virginia and Washington, D.C., I worked with some incredibly talented managers and owners but did not seek out mentorship or coaching, which I regret. I certainly learned a lot, had amazing experiences and grew in my career, but I know that with the right mentor I would have shortened the learning curve and had greater success.

Since moving to Georgia in 2002, I've had an amazing woman mentor me personally. Joan Millar has become a friend, confidant, and teacher in my spiritual and personal development walk. I truly can say that because of her I'm the friend, wife, and mother that I am today. She's strong in her faith and took me from a dark place in my early 30s to today and has been an incredible resource, guide, and inspiration. While most mentors are for professional development, if your life and spirit are not in a good place, then the best teaching will not land in fertile ground and grow. I believe because of work we did together and clearing away some bad habits and misguided beliefs, we made room for good teachings and good habits to develop. As humans, and especially as entrepreneurs, we are constantly evolving and growing. Attracting the good and discarding the bad is ongoing. Having a strong faith has been key for me. There are times being an entrepreneur is very lonely and very scary. Faith is the only weapon I have found to fight those internal and external battles.

I have a variety of teachers in my professional walk today. There's so much to learn and so much to develop. Good Reading is important. Every entrepreneur should read *Think and Grow Rich* by Napoleon Hill, *How to Win Friends and Influence People* by Dale Carnegie, *Getting Things Done* by David Allen, *When Things Fall Apart; Heart Advice for Difficult Times* by Pema Chodron, *As a Man Thinketh* by James Allen and *Eat That Frog!: 21 Great Ways to Stop Procrastinating and Get More Done in Less Time* by Brian Tracy. There are countless other books depending on your field and your own level of personal development. Ongoing education and learning is critical in any entrepreneurial field.

Has being in your industry helped you to expand to other industries?

Yes. When we started Oakwood Occasions in 2008 I didn't have a plan and was acting on instinct and need to support our family so we focused on catering and food preparation. As the business grew and developed, we ventured into coffee and vending services, opened a coffee shop and café in a government office building to include an internship program with a local high school for graduating students with special needs, and expanded our event planning into conferences, parades, festivals, and other vendor and attendance-driven events. We expanded our offerings to brides and personal events, as well as added a direct sales company with an incredible coffee and tea line, Organo. The last three years with a network marketing company in our umbrella of hospitality offerings has been very rewarding and profitable! All of this has also lead to public speaking, articles, and now the opportunity to be an author.

If someone was to come to you for help, what would be the first thing you would tell them in regards to getting started in your industry?

I've interviewed and hired so many people in the last several years that have planned a small event or seen the finished event and want to get into the event planning industry. When they get the full picture of the mental and physical work required to produce an event, they are surprised and not equipped or ready to handle the whole package. I always recommend getting into a company that is similar to your goals or will give you experience in a new area of business or growth. If you don't have experience to bring to the table, an internship opportunity is ideal. When my business was growing, and I needed help but didn't quite have the profitability to bring on the right staff, I offered internships from a local college, which was a great opportunity to me to teach what I know and give time and experience to those interested in the field. Many of those interns have gone on to start their own businesses or they saw the complete picture of event planning and have adapted their goals. I had one employee that had only worked in the industry for one venue and didn't understand the physical and mental requirements of off-site event planning and catering. After working one shift, she realized she wasn't prepared or able to work in this sector of the industry. Every learning experience can get you closer to your goals or help you to define your goals if you are open. Learning what you do not love or are not interested in pursuing is just as important in furthering your knowledge and career. It is far better to intern and give of your time before investing a great deal of money and work into a business, equipment, or education that won't serve you. Attend as many events as you can. Take notes on what works, what was pleasing as a guest, what made sense, and what challenges you witnessed. Event planning can appear glamorous and fun. At times it certainly is, but there is a *lot* of hard work that precedes the fun! When the challenges arise, which they will, it is only experience that will help you navigate to a plan B seamlessly and effectively for your clients, so the more experience you can gather the better you will be equipped to become "MacGyver" on site when you need to make adjustments for venue, weather, equipment, vendors, attendees, and whatever new challenge that the current event may offer!

Outside of working (in your industry) what is your favorite thing to do?
Spend time with my husband and children. We had kids later in life, and for that I'm so grateful! I believe I appreciate the balance in life more and understand that everything and every moment is a choice.

Do you provide coaching or resources to anyone who wants to further educate themselves in your industry?
Yes, I've talked about internships and teaching and guiding on that level. We also have developed a more detailed event planning coaching program for potential EPs who may want to own their own business in the future or want to get the knowledge needed to be their own event hosts. We currently offer our vendors training by conference call and webinar to give them the best information and guidelines for success both at the events we produce and to have the right kind of follow-up lead system to generate profitable results.

Is there anything you don't necessarily love about the industry?
The hardest element to handle and overcome is unrealistic expectations of clients. As it relates to food service, the greatest area of misunderstanding is the cost to produce a quality catered event. I've spent a great deal of time working with clients to find the right compromises when vision and budget balance. There's also a common misconception about cooking on a large scale. Because most people cook for themselves on some level, they may assume they understand what cooking for 25 or 2500 might entail. Again, lots of working with clients and

education! As a beginning entrepreneur it's hard not to feel like you have to get every job, every proposal. You have to learn that not every job is right for your business, and not every dollar is worth earning. Your time and experience have value. There has to be the right fit for you and your clients. I've dealt with clients or competitors using our complimentary consultation model to gather information only to find they used it to further their interests or to undercut pricing. An unfortunate element of the industry is to have some cutthroat competition or the impression that do-it-yourself is a better idea than paying a professional. Experience prevents some of these issues from having a great effect overall, but it still happens. I still like to offer our consultations because of the customizations that we bring to events, but it's a risk that opens the door for my time being undervalued or unappreciated. I am so grateful for the amazing clients who more than make up for the few negative experiences!

What favorite marketing strategies have you used to help with building your business?

1. **Word of Mouth/Networking Events:** Attending networking events and sharing about the business and our offerings was our first and still very effective type of marketing. Events, especially weddings and family events, are very personal. Clients love a personal relationship. All of our early clients came from direct referrals, which are still a strong part of our marketing efforts.

2. **Facebook and other Social Media Marketing:** We were fortunate that Facebook launched and gained popularity at the same time we began our business. By posting pictures and information about our events, we were able to take word of mouth referrals to another level and to another dimension. We've got an active presence on Facebook, Twitter, LinkedIn, Pinterest, Instagram, and now Periscope. Some with more success than others, but clearly social media marketing is a necessary component of events, marketing, and branding.

3. **Email Marketing:** This marketing tool has been the most effective with our vendor and attendance-driven events to communicate with those that will be sponsors and vendors and to share upcoming events. We have a monthly newsletter that is one of our best ways to grow and expand from event to event.

What are 3 books that you recommend for success in your industry?

- *Who Moved My Cheese?* - Spencer Johnson
- *The Wedding Book* - Mindy Weiss
- *Delivering Happiness: A Path to Profits, Passion and Purpose* - Tony Hsieh.

These are just a few and will touch on very different aspects of the event industry. There are other great resources within each category of event management as well.

If there was one thing you may have done differently in your industry when you got started, what would it have been?

Seven years ago we could have reduced our learning curve by having a business plan and a model for the type of business and events for which we would strive to provide services. However, I also believe that we walked out on faith and certain people, places, and opportunities came our way because of that faith walk—and because we didn't have a plan other than to provide for our family and provide for our clients. By keeping those goals in the forefront, I believe that the business has grown in ways that came from blessings and from a place of service to others. I know that many mistakes have also been made along the way like money spent from an emotional decision rather than from sound business sense, equipment or products purchases that didn't show a good return on investment, and things that "seemed like a good idea at the time." We've managed countless events over the years where I misjudged the monetary investment in products, people, and preparation and not earned profits, given away samples, or provided discounts because it might be a good promotional opportunity. Each of these mistakes has been a learning experience. One thing I can always provide for my clients is the assurance that the same mistakes won't be made again! Each of my brides has the benefit of the 25-35 weddings we do per year and knowing what works and what doesn't so the best decisions are made! Over time, we developed better clarity in our own vision and made some significant changes to our business model and systems last year to better tend to our ongoing success and our clients.

What is your favorite quote?
"For I know the plans I have for you, declares the Lord, plans to prosper you and not harm you, plans to give you hope and a future." —**Jeremiah 29:11**

Special Thanks to the following

Aimee Oczkowski
Owner/Distributor, Aim4GoodHealth, LLC with Juice Plus
Facebook.com/Aim4GoodHealthLLC

Amanda Dutton
Licensed Therapist, Healthy Life Counseling, LLC
Facebook.com/HealthyLifeCounseling

Brian Hay
Owner, BnB Enterprises, Amway IBO
Facebook.com/BriansOneStopShop

Carol Neal
Co-Founder, Atlanta Business Spotlight
Facebook.com/AtlantaBusinessSpotlight

Cherry Lobo
Owner, Cherry-O the Clown and Friends
Facebook.com/Cherry-O-The-Clown-126137637405257

Debbie Loveless
Anti-Aging Coach, Enagic – Kangan Water Specialist
Facebook.com/Debbie.Rivers.Loveless

Elissa Mitchell
Independent Distributor, Total Life Changes
Facebook.com/Elissa.Mitchell.73

Gene Kerley
Realtor, Keller Williams
Facebook.com/Gene.S.Kerley

Jill Mashburn
General Manager, Northside Homecrafters, Inc.
Facebook.com/NorthsideHomecrafters

Joshua Smith
Gold Executive, Essante Organics
Facebook.com/StrategicOrganics

Karen Seward
Owner, Karen's Coffee Corner
Facebook.com/Karen.Seward.98

Leah Brown
Independent Distributor, Arbonne
Facebook.com/Leah.H.Brown.5

Lisa Bailey
Independent Distributor, Premier Designs Jewelry
Facebook.com/Lisa.S.Bailey.52

Lori Sorensen
Independent Distributor, Thirty-One Gifts
Facebook.com/LorisBagLadies

Lynne Booth
Owner, Sweet P Flowers
Facebook.com/Sweet-P-Flowers-132364530139348

Marilyn Davis
Owner/Editor, Two Drops of Ink
Facebook.com/TwoDropsofInk

Monica Caras
Owner, Club Z! In-Home Tutoring Service
Facebook.com/ClubZBuford

Robin Hill
Owner, Virtual Office Assist, LLC
Facebook.com/VirtualOfficeAssist

Stephanie Combes
C.O.O, Instatricity
Facebook.com/Instatricity

Whitney Delong
Owner/Coach, Whitney Delong Health & Fitness Coaching
Facebook.com/WhitneyDelongFitness

Diana Lynn Perez

Industry - Insurance
Instagram.com/IamDianaPerez
Twitter.com/DianaBBLA
www.businessandbalance.org

Diana Lyn Perez, is an author, speaker, and insurance business strategist. Diana has been the owner of Perez Insurance Professionals, LLC for 4 years, and since December 2014 is the CEO/Founder of Business and Balance Ladies of Atlanta, Inc. Diana is a seasoned expert at all things business, sales, and networking. Working in the insurance industry for over 14 years has provided continuous education opportunities, sales trainings, success, and personal growth for Diana, In the past, she has worked for the number one world risk insurance brokers, Marsh and McLennan, among other high-end insurance brokers. Combined with her vast knowledge and the burning desire to elevate others in the community, Ms. Perez's skills and mindset afforded her the ability and expertise to generate a massive growth in sales in premiums on single policies in excess of $10,000 on many of her clients in the affluent market. Continuously educating herself, she has become the business and insurance expert to many clients, friends, and networking partners.

Diana found great passion in connecting with women, helping them grow by providing expert advice, trainings, and balancing business with fun and rest. Since founding BBLA in December of 2014, Business & Balance Ladies of Atlanta has grown to more than 3,200 ladies through her Facebook group platform in a little more than twelve months! Last, Diana has been noted to have hundreds of attendees at her events, workshops and monthly meetings. Many clients and members have regarded her efforts a phenomenal improvement in the Atlanta business market. Ms. Perez offers regular strategy sales and networking sessions, workshops for professionals, insurance agents, and business owners, as well as effective empowerment and teaching events. Business & Balance is unlike any other entrepreneur organization in Georgia.

How long have you been in your industry?
I was 21 years old when I began in the industry in 1998. I did not graduate from college. At the time, I moved out of my mother's home and needed to find a "job" for my new apartment. I started walking around my new neighborhood, and

I found an insurance agency. I walked in and asked if they were hiring, and they were! I have now been working hard in the industry for more than fifteen plus years! Time has flown by. I am grateful for that small agency teaching and my willingness to listen.

Why did you get into your industry?
I actually stumbled upon it, as I mentioned prior. I did not know at that age what I was going to do in my career. I wanted to help people and to grow, I knew that much. Lucky for me, insurance does just that. Insurance educates you and puts you in the community to help others protect their risk. I interviewed at this amazing insurance agency now called Mayes Insurance Group as a receptionist and I grew fast; the rest is history. I went on to manage other agencies and own my own six-figure agency.

When it comes to being an entrepreneur, what do you love most about it?
I love the freedom of being an entrepreneur and the legacy I will leave. There is nothing like being able to leave for an appointment not needing to let anyone know that I have to go. The legacy I am leaving as an entrepreneur is that I work hard, I apply simple but sometimes hard practices daily, and I get to live comfortably and leave a legacy that my family is proud of.

What would you consider the pros about being in your industry?
Hands down the residual income, the opportunity to teach clients, and the multiple streams you can get from being an insurance agent such as teaching continuing education classes, sales trainings, and the like to make additional income. I'm able to sell other products with other companies that I myself don't offer.

Were you required to make any financial and/or time investments to get started?
Honestly, I had only $1,800 to invest. I had my license already, but needed to rent an office, purchase what is called E&O insurance for my agency, a printer, computer, miscellaneous materials, quoting systems, etc.

What is the average income in your industry?
With an average pay as a new agent of $23.01 per hour, it is triple the Georgia state minimum wage of $7.50, according to the United States Department of Labor. That is only accounting for selling insurance on a base, not including any commission you can make. That is $47,860 per year. According to Glassdoor, an Allstate agency owner makes anywhere from $100k to $126k a year not including bonuses. As an independent agent, you can make more. I am living proof of that.

When it comes to success in your industry, what are 3 main tips you would give to those interested in doing what you do?

1. **Pound the pavement/network** - Everyone is not privy to having a network where insurance sales "fall" into your lap. Get out, plan your day, meet with plenty of businesses and people who need better insurance products than they currently have, and market!

2. **Continuously educate yourself** - Take every opportunity to perfect your craft. Study, read, and take classes for the CPCU, CIA designations, etc. to educate yourself more and more every chance you get. Be the expert, and people will come to you for your expertise.

3. **Never be afraid to ask for the close!** - Be confident in who you are and your ability to teach a client the importance of having insurance. The security it provides is hands down the best any consumer can purchase. Go for the close. Have rebuttals, choose wise words, *listen,* and then ask, "Would you like to use a credit card or choose auto check draft?" I mean it. People who have low closing ratios won't make the type of money we successful agents can and have made. You can do it!

When actively working in your industry, what does a day (week) look like for you?
I plan my schedule to what benefits me most financially. One day it may be a regular 9 a.m. to 5 p.m. at the office, selling and

servicing with an hour for networking. Tuesday, I may be out networking for four hours that day and coming back to quote some business for another six hours. Wednesday may be that I am creating marketing plans and materials for three hours, then cold calling for an hour. It all depends on what is most effective. But I plan my day, and I stick to it as best I can.

Do you have a mentor?

I had several mentors as from the time I became a new agent up until I became an agency owner. The only reason I didn't have a mentor when I owned an agency is that I wasn't familiar with anyone that was in my state (fairly new to the state) who was extremely successful (making $250,000 or more), and I didn't make any connections in that. That was an error of mine. But I am a woman who learns by hard work. I made it happen because I educated myself, and I listened and remembered what I was taught in the 10 years *prior* to owning my agency. Find a mentor in any case!

Has being in your industry helped you to expand to other industries?

Yes! I learned when I moved to a state that I basically knew no one. I had to learn how to find my niche market and how to network and build key relationships. That in turn, got me plenty of great referrals. I own two businesses now and am working on a third. I am a sales strategist for men and women, but own a women's professional organization that grew very fast and is expanding in several states. I am creating another online program for new and old insurance agents to vastly expand their businesses. I am an author and speaker. This industry has blessed me in so many ways! I can do the same for you.

If someone was to come to you for help, what would be the first thing you would tell them in regards to getting started in your industry?

Have you ever been told "no," and did you move on from that "no?" If so, insurance is for you! If you can handle rejection but still expect reward, you are for this industry!

Outside of working (in your industry) what is your favorite thing to do?
I love to host events. I empower people, I teach people, and I serve, and it's one of the best feelings in the world.

Do you provide coaching or resources to anyone who wants to further educate themselves in your industry?
Yes, I teach and provide resources for a new insurance agent to be the best they can be in the industry and make the money they want! I teach seasoned agents and agency owners how I came to where I am in such a short period of time and how they can get back on track or increase sales by completing some changes in their businesses.

Is there anything you don't necessarily love about the industry?
The only thing I don't love is when people cancel! But I have found the key to when they cancel, you sell two more and get your money back plus another! Keep moving; sell more!

What favorite marketing strategies have you used to help with building your business?
- Networking (I network about four hours or more a week.)
- I make creative marketing materials and go to businesses in my niche market to solicit too. It has always worked for me.
- I cross sell. If the client only has one policy, I offer additional lines and let them see the value in more products.—problem to solution.

What are 3 books that you recommend for success in your industry?

- *How I Built a $37 Million Insurance Agency In Less Than 7 Years* - Darren Sugiyama
- Your state specific insurance property & casualty, life & health manuals! These are the bible in our world.

- *Insurance Commander: How to Sell Property and Casualty Business Insurance* - Baxter Dunbar

What is your favorite quote?
"There is no royal flower-strewn path to success. And if there is, I have not found it for if I have accomplished anything in life it is because I have been willing to work hard." —Madam C.J. Walker

Special thanks to the following

Elisha Batson
President - BELAN

JoAnn Dean MSW, BCC
Master Social Worker, Board Certified Coach
The JD Experience, LLC
Facebook.com/SisterCircleRetreat

Selma Gilcrease
CEO & Founder
Sparkle & Shine Cleaning Services,LLC
Facebook.com/SparkeshinecleaningservicesLLC

Tomeka Mark
CEO & Life Coach
The Mark Agency, LLC
http:/Facebook.com/BrokenTreasureMinistry

Elissa Mitchell
Health & Wellness Distributor
Total Life Changes
Facebook.com/Elissa.Mitchell.73

Monique Williams
CEO & Founder
Rock Ya Bella Boutique
Facebook.com/rockyabellaboutique

Rosemary Willingham
President & CEO

LifeCycles Strategies
Facebook.com/LifeCyclesEnrichment

Kim Kennedy
Health & Nutrition Coach
Facebook.com/Kim-Kennedys-Health-Wellness-Coaching

Candice Barnes
CEO & Master Baker
Sweetly Done by Candi
Facebook.com/sweetlydonebycandi

Lisa Lashaye Burt
Independent Business Owner
Total Life Changes
Facebook.com/lisa.l.burt

Frances Whitten
Associate/Consultant - Isagenix
Facebook.com/xcdecatur

Sandy Hoeffner
CEO & Wellness Advocate - Awe-Inspiring Solutions
Facebook.com/awe-inspiringsolutions

Kim Kennedy Title
Health & Nutrition Coach
Facebook.com/Kim-Kennedys-Health-Wellness

Aurea McGarry

Industry - Home Based Business
Instagram.com/AureaMcgarry
Facebook.com/Aurea.Mcgarry
Persicope.tv/AureaMcGgarry
Twitter.com/AureaMcGarry
Google.com/+AureaMcGarryLegacy
Linkedin.com/in/AureaMcgarry
www.AureaMcgarry.com

A direct sales master trainer, Emmy Award winning TV show host/producer/director, author, best-selling co-author, speaker, emcee, and founder of the very popular Live Your Legacy Summit event series.

Aurea McGarry, AKA the Legacy Maker® is a former Pink Cadillac senior sales director winning hundreds of awards, diamonds, prizes and eight free company cars, including two pink Cadillacs and one black BMW she earned in her first 30 days in Visalus. A successful leader for more than thirty years, her innovated sales and recruiting techniques for direct sellers are some of the most sought after in the industry. She has shared her higher income strategies with over a million consultants nationwide in dozens of companies including Mary Kay Inc., The Trump Network, Visalus, Origami Owl, and Christian Bling. She's been personally trained by legends such as Mary Kay Ash, Zig Ziglar, John Maxwell, Mark Victor Hansen, the co-author of the Chicken Soup book series, and Jairek Robbins just to name a few.

Aurea not only rose to top positions in many direct sales companies, she did it despite some very traumatic situations including escaping a very abusive husband, using her free company car as her getaway car for her and her then-five-year-old daughter, Angelica, and achieving her greatest success during and after her grueling battle over cancer, where the doctors had to remove half of her left lung and part of her right lung, along with removing her left vocal cord nerve. She was told it would be impossible for her to speak above a faint whisper ever again. It was a diagnosis that would stop most entrepreneurs who speak and teach for a living dead in their tracks, but that was not an option for her, and she achieved many of her greatest accomplishments and awards during those extremely tough times. She's become a master coach, empowering others with her tried and true skills to do the same thing as she knows all too well that life happens while you're making other plans, and tough times should not stop anyone from reaching their ultimate goals and dreams.

Born and raised in Manhattan as an actor, singer, and dancer, she currently lives in North Georgia with her prince charming husband, Brian, and their youngest daughter, Alyssa, along with their beloved pets—two dogs, a great pyrenees and a golden retriever/Australian shepherd mix and a fat lovable stray cat that found his way into their home and hearts.

How long have you been in your industry?
I have been in the direct selling industry since 1990. I spent the better part of 20 years working it as my full-time career and full-time income as a super achiever in national sales, recruiting, and team leading with very large personal down lines, multiple free company cars, more than 12 carats of diamonds earned, bonuses, awards, and more as a top 1 percent leader and national trainer. I have shared my experiences, success strategies, and expert techniques with more than a million consultants and fellow leaders nationwide and in dozens of popular direct selling companies. Although I am not currently in the sales force of any one company at the moment, I am actively coaching private and group master classes through my Legacy Maker® series to help those who want to learn my tried and true strategies to move quickly up their career paths and avoid making mistakes that could cause them to waste valuable time and money.

Why did you get into your industry?
I joined my first direct sales company to earn a free company car, which was much needed in my one car household at that time, and to make enough money to put my then-4-year-old daughter into Christian private school. I had no idea this industry would change my life forever and rescue me financially and physically. I earned my first of eight free company cars within my very first year and used it as a getaway car to escape a domestically abusive husband, now ex-husband, and I earned more than enough money in my sales and team commissions to put my daughter in private school, which was my dream that I turned into an achievable goal. With a specific goal date, all things can be accomplished if you then work backwards to make them a reality.

149

When it comes to being an entrepreneur, what do you love most about it?
What I absolutely love the most about being an entrepreneur is having a life, a lifestyle, choices, financial freedom and being my own boss, working when I want to, and being able to always take off anytime to be with my family and friends for all the important moments and milestones. It has allowed me to *live* a legacy, not just survive a life pay check to pay check helping to make someone else's dreams come true.

Only in direct sales can you build your own higher income lifestyle while mentoring a team of other successful people who work full or part time running their own business, lives, and chosen schedules, and they are able to create their own 6-figure income and lifestyle to reach their financial dreams as well if they choose to do so. It is such a winning industry for those who do it and work it the right way. It is hard work, but so is anything and everything that is profitable and worth doing.

What would you consider the pros about being in your industry?
There are too many pros to mention in this short chapter, but if you read the book *"Rich Dad, Poor Dad"* you will get a fuller idea of the positive impact having a direct selling business in your life can truly have. It works for you 24/7 while you sleep, travel, and work on other passions in your life and so much more.

Some of my favorite pros to running a home-based business are the wonderful and much-needed tax advantages available to you, although they can change year to year, which is why it is vital that you not only have a great CPA but that he or she is an expert in filing taxes for home based businesses specifically. Do not make the mistake many people make thinking that all CPAs are the same and can do the job. Au contraire, my friends; I learned that lesson the hard way. The best advice I can give you on this is to ask several of the highest up line leaders in your state, who have been earning at least a six figure income for over three years, who their CPA is. It can be that easy. Get a few referrals and interview them all and choose the one you like best, knowing that they all are referred to you by people in your industry, who make a lot of money and you respect their opinions because they are where you want to be financially.

Now I will tell you who I use because she is a godsend! The smartest and most honest woman in the world, who knows the tax business better than anyone I have ever met, came to me very highly recommended by several celebrities that I know and have worked with. Her name is Dawn Brolin CPA, MSA as seen on MSNBC Business, www.DawnBrolin.com. Now, I won't try to sell you anything in this book, but this is such an important subject that can make or break your business, as many small businesses fail every year due to bad money management and/or having the wrong CPA on their team that I have to at least mention Dawn to you and to all of my clients just in case she can help you as much as she helps me and all of her clients. Everyone ends up asking me who does my taxes anyway, so I get this out of the way right up front. So there you go. Enjoy, and she is as funny as she is smart—trust me!

Another great pro of being in a home-based business is that you are in business for yourself but definitely not by yourself. You enter into a company that is set up to support you in every way, and for you to succeed, all you have to do is plug in, learn, work, and get paid. You don't have to be the inventor of a great product yourself or invest millions of dollars into setting up the company yourself from the ground up, you simply sign up, get trained and GO! This has made many people very wealthy, so why not you next?

One of my other favorite reasons for loving the direct selling industry is that it literally saved my life financially when I was diagnosed with cancer in 1999, and I had been working full time for three years prior in a direct sales company in a top leadership position. It was on my birthday that year when the doctors gave me the bad news that I had cancer in my chest cavity, and they needed to go in and do exploratory surgery to see how bad it was and how many organs it may have infected. Not the birthday present a girl wants when she turns 38 years old, but these were my cards and I had to play them. God was in control anyway, so I wasn't worried. After I signed off giving the surgeon carte blanche to do whatever needed to be done in the operating room to save my life when they opened me up, I was no less shocked to hear the news in the ICU when I awoke from a very long intense surgery. They told me that the cancer was curable, non-Hodgkin's lymphoma, but that they had to remove half of my left lung, part of my right lung, my thymus gland, the lining around my heart, and the left thoracic nerve to my vocal cord. They had to disconnect half of my diaphragm, and they told me I would never be able to speak above a faint whisper ever again. Well, that was certainly not going to be conducive to my direct selling career and my public speaking, teaching, and making sales and training calls on a daily basis. But I gave all that to God and concentrated on the next step—chemotherapy. Which brings me to a huge pro of being successful in a direct sales company: even if you cannot work personally due to a tragic time in your life, you can still have people working in your business in your down lines that enable you to maintain and/or increase your income even while you can't show up in person. In addition, you will not have to worry about clocking into a job that could hand you a pink slip at any moment if you miss too many days of work or are too sick to accomplish what your boss needs you to do.

I was so extremely sick during my many months on chemo that I could have never been able to keep a regular job during that grueling year. I threw up eighteen times a day for ten days straight after every single chemo treatment every three weeks, but thanks to my hard work for the three years that led up to my cancer battle, my large team kept on working during the time I was down, and I was able to actually make even higher team commission checks than normal due to their extra efforts during that intense year when I was fighting for my life.

You see, direct sales can also be your extended family who truly cares about you, and you care about them, and it becomes more than just a pay check; lives can be changed for the better. Having no fear of losing your income no matter what circumstances or tragedy come your way is possible if you treat your direct selling business like a proper business right now. Working hard now will keep you from worrying about your income when the inevitable rainy days come because you took it upon yourself to ensure your financial security, and that is what a home base business can give you: financial stability, security and hope for your future.

Were you required to make any financial and/or time investments to get started?
Of course I had to invest time and money into joining all of the home-based businesses I entered into, as I don't know of any legal business venture that doesn't cost time and some money to join them. Nothing worthwhile comes for free. But as I mentioned before, the cost of joining a home-based company is so little compared to starting up your very own company from scratch, which costs thousands and even millions to bring to the consumers. Most home-based business starter kits range from $50 to $299 and the cost of buying optional inventory varies greatly since some companies have no inventory to stock up on because they are a service rather than a retail product while others do suggest having inventory on your shelves to sell on the spot to your customers at parties and vendor shows like cosmetics, jewelry, and wellness products. In direct sales it is always your choice how much money, if any, that you invest in supplies and products in that particular company.

Personally, I always loved investing in the products when I joined because I have found that having a large quantity and variety of the products on hand at my parties, shows, and vendor events made my sales much higher than taking orders and making the customer wait a week or so for delivery. I loved on the spot selling, but that is just my preference. There is no right or wrong way in this department, you do what makes you comfortable and what fits into your lifestyle and budget. Both ways can create wealth for you if you do it consistently and give great customer service at all times.

Also, find out the buyback rules of the company you are interested in as most of them have a money back guarantee on unsold products should the day come that you want to quit the company and still have too many items to sell by yourself. Be aware of their time limits and how much they give you back on the dollar as sometimes it is a better deal for you to have a big blow out sale yourself rather than selling it back for less money to the company. Read the fine print in every agreement before you sign up.

What are the statistics of success in your industry?
The direct selling business is a $32 billion a year industry in the US alone and over $114 billion worldwide that changes lives for the better—though sometimes for the worse if you are not careful and you don't treat it like a business and give it the respect, attention, and excellent work ethics it deserves and requires. Direct selling is the marketing and selling of products directly to consumers away from a fixed retail location. Most direct selling associations around the world require their members to abide by a code of conduct towards a fair partnership both with customers and salesmen. Also, most national direct selling associations are represented in the World Federation of Direct Selling Associations (WFDSA). 81.8 percent are women mainly in the age ranges of thirty to forty-six years old with eighteen to twenty-nine-year-olds accounting for about 13 percent of those women. According to Direct Sellers Statistics, 84 percent of them meet their monthly financial expectations, and 91 percent of them said that direct selling is much more profitable with less amount of work than running an independent business on your own.

The best thing about joining a direct selling company is that everything is already set up and done for you, so you as an individual you don't have the extremely high start-up cost involved setting up a new company and all that goes into creating, distributing, and marketing it nationwide and worldwide. Lawyer and website development fees alone make it out of reach for the average person. So joining a company that allows you to jump in for very little cost and start selling and building a team right away is a huge benefit that can be a very lucrative 6-figure income relatively quickly for those who embrace it and work it with 100 percent passion just as if they created the entire company themselves.

Direct sales companies' career paths are set up for people to succeed and rise up the promotional ladders to a higher income level. The only problem is that most people give up after they approach their family and friends, and they never move on to strangers, who are their real customers and their real future. I hesitate to talk about the average success rate of people in this industry because I would have never risen up to the top if I knew the average person usually quits too soon. I loved that I had no idea who succeeded and who failed in this business, all I knew was that I had to succeed personally and that I had a short time frame to do that in as my daughter was turning 5 and entering into kindergarten in 12 short months, so I had no time to waste learning national statistics. I spent all my time learning and working my business instead, and it paid off in spades. I highly suggest you do the same; stay focused on *you*, not the rise or fall of others.

My number one tip is to hang onto your up line leaders, as they are where you want to be. If possible, invest in a professional coach as it will be your best investment ever if you choose your coach wisely. This is applicable no matter what field you're in now or planning on entering into in the future.

What is the average income in your industry?

A Direct Selling News Study Conducted by Harris Poll in 2014 it showed that 7% made nothing at all, 27 percent made less than $1,000, 51 percent earned $1,000 to $49,999, and 15 percent polled earned $50,000 or more annually. But you know me; I don't go by national averages in my life because I don't believe in being average or working like an average-minded entrepreneur. The only way to experience greatness is to put your blinders on and go full steam ahead in the direction you know you are called to run in and not to worry about what the average "Joe" accomplishes or doesn't accomplish in your field because they're *not* you! Use your God-given talents and abilities to their fullest and watch God blow your mind on how great your results can be when others around you are barely getting by or quitting. That has nothing to do with you or your potential results, now does it? You don't want to be average either, so don't think twice about who is failing in your industry; none of that means anything to your future.

When I first began in direct sales in 1990, I was very young and naive and didn't know one thing about the field I entered into, which was cosmetics, but I knew I needed that free car quickly and the extra money for Christian school for my little girl. So I not only never missed my weekly meetings, I sat in the front row and did everything my up line told me to do without fail, and many times I did it with her help and support. With all that in mind, I had no idea that the entire room of women had been attending these local training meetings for almost 10 years prior and no one in that room had ever won a company car or moved up into a leadership role. When I came in on day one as a rookie, green behind the ears, I didn't know anyone else's sales stats or if anyone had struggles along the way. I simply took action right away, sat in the front row, worked hard as a fast learner, and set my sights on winning everything offered to us, knowing that would lead me to where I ultimately wanted and needed to be financially. So I won every weekly prize, every crown for queen of sales and queen of recruiting, and went to the car dealership in only 12 short months to pick up my free company car as the first woman in that room to achieve that success level. I had no clue that I was not average at that moment, all I knew is that I needed it all and worked very hard towards my goals daily, and that enabled me to *surpass everyone else in my path*. I exceeded the average statistics which is what great work ethics will get you every time! Ignorance is definitely better in cases like this. Don't look to the left or to the right; keep your eyes focused on your race and run it as fast as you can. The only person you are competing with is you.

When it comes to success in your industry, what are 3 main tips you would give to those interested in doing what you do.

1. Love the product or services that you sell, because if you passionately love them yourself, your life will be easier than if you simply like the products or tolerate them. If you love what you do, you will never work

156

another day in your life. So be very on point when it comes to joining any company, knowing that you must be sold out yourself on the product or services you provide your clients with, because people, especially women, will see right through you if you try and fake enthusiasm. That is why I tell people to quit a company and join another one they are more passionate about if I feel they are unhappy with the company's ethics, career plan, products, ingredients, or something else, because you must be completely in love with all of the company you represent in order to truly get up to the top in a timely manner and be successful and happy. Loving and believing in what you do does make a big difference, so find that perfect company for you, and don't be afraid to shop around until you do. There is no shortage of choices in America and in most parts of the world now too. That is one reason 80 percent of direct sellers are looking for a better home base business to join right now.

2. My second tip is to have or learn great time management skills. When you are in business for yourself, you are your own boss, which can also work against you if you don't execute your own weekly plan sheets and put yourself on a winning work schedule. Think to yourself often, would you fire yourself for lack of productivity? You're the boss, so be the boss! The beauty of a home-based business is that you can have it all—God first, family second, and career third while earning a wonderful income, but it does take discipline, consistent work, and good strategies in place, which are learned skills. Having a good up line and or a good coach helps keep people on task. Whether it is a workout coach, life coach, or business coach, being accountable to another person is always recommended. It can be too easy to not be hard on yourself at home, and it is easy to get distracted working at home with family interruptions, personal calls coming in, dogs barking,

door bells ringing, etc. The list of ways to procrastinate at home are endless.

3. My third tip would be to not to quit too soon. Remember I told you that 80 percent of direct sellers are actively looking for a better, more exciting company to move over to so don't be that person. Do your homework first so you choose the right company that fits your personality and interests the best so that you can give yourself the best chance to succeed from day one. Once you have carefully selected the company you believe in most, work it with your whole heart for at least four ninety-day cycles in a row—which comes out to twelve months. This does not mean you have to work it all of the time, it does mean you set aside the amount of time you want to dedicate to it daily, weekly, monthly, and quarterly, and then plan your work and work your plan without giving yourself permission to quit until you have worked a full twelve months in a row, part-time or full-time. My ninety-day plans are very successful when my clients create their own and take action with ninety-day goals on their goal posters. This gives them a much better success rate because we all have those terrible weeks happen which could lead to getting discouraged or even quitting when obstacles come along, but if you're steadfast on a ninety-day cycle you created for yourself, then when day forty-five comes and you have had everything hit the fan that week and you want to throw your starter kit out your car window going seventy miles an hour down the interstate, you don't give in to that temptation because you have yourself on a ninety-day success plan, and you don't allow yourself to stop for any reason until you reach the 90th day. By that day, you will have achieved many good days and are well on your way to your next ninety-day cycle, knowing that you promised yourself to give it one full year, no exceptions, and that great things take time to cultivate and generate fruits of your labor.

If home-based businesses were actually get rich quick schemes, then we would all be rich, but they are not, so time, energy, consistency, and good old fashioned stick-to-it determination is needed in this industry, as it is not for everyone and not for the faint of heart or for those who would rather not be their very own best and toughest boss.

When actively working in your industry, what does a day (week) look like for you?
My very busy days and weeks are always planned in advance on Sunday nights with a weekly plan sheet. Everything went on my very specific color coded weekly plan sheet (my color coding is another subject for another time) including, lunches with clients and or team members, product selling parties, vendor events, recruiting interviews, training classes, meetings, time with family and friends, errands to run, and all outgoing calls had specific time slots at the beginning of every weekday. Those calls include calls to current customers as well as to generate new ones and follow up calls, team training calls, interview calls, etc. My weeks were and still are very organized, and everything gets written down even if I take a week off, which is a great benefit of running your own business—you rule your own time completely. So when I was in high gear moving up the ladders, I had lots of business appointments holding product shows, company interviews for new team members over coffee or lunch, training classes that I taught to new and advanced sales people on my team and on others' teams, as well as many times I was a national trainer for others in addition to my own down lines.

When I was working it full-time, I averaged two to three selling parties every single week, booking more than that knowing that cancellations happen frequently in this industry; it is just the way it is. Life happens, so you must work the numbers game, which is to book more appointments than you want to actually hold each and every week.

I would always book at least one recruiting interview from each of those parties, giving me an average of 3 recruiting interviews to hold each week to grow my down line consistently.

As a leader holding a high position, I would also hold a weekly training and sales meeting every single Monday night from 6:00 p.m. – 9:00 p.m. without fail for 15 years, and they were the main ingredient to my and my strong team's successes over the years together.

Saturdays would either be a monthly fashion show hosted by me or another leader in the company when I was selling cosmetics or a day off for me to enjoy a fun family outing or a big vendor show. I would usually book one or two each month, and they were often on a Saturday, like a bridal show, for example, which was a great place to meet potential new customers and team members at my vendor booths. I love vendor booths; they can be a huge part of growing any type of business, and it is one of my favorite things to teach people how to work them successfully as there are many dos and don'ts on this subject in order to get the best possible results from each show.

There was always plenty of time for family dinners, shopping with my daughters, travel, and lots of fun times making memories with friends and family, but we were all a team, and when the end of the month would come or there was a big deadline to win a new car or big promotion or bonus, we all knew it was crunch time for me, and I would have less time for fun that week or that month. My family was a big part of my goals and accomplishments, so even during those really intense work weeks, we still were in it together, and it was still part of family time. We worked together for a common goal so no one felt deprived or neglected. The family that works together also enjoys playing together. So we all constantly celebrated the winnings, free cars, and the lifestyle that our hard work allowed us to have by running our chosen home-based businesses as a team.

Do you have a mentor?
After so many years in this industry, yes of course I have had many mentors along the way. Some have been the higher achievers in the companies I worked in, and others have been paid coaches I hired to help me get to the next level of success. One of the best tips I ever learned has worked for me in every

single business I have ever been in as well as producing my TV shows and Live Your Legacy Summits, and it is a famous tip from Mary Kay Ash, who empowered millions of people during her lifetime. She was one of my favorite mentors of all time, and I had the honor and pleasure of being trained by her in person several times before she died on Nov. 22, 2001. She learned one of her most famous winning strategies from a true story about Charles Schwab, president of Bethlehem Steel, and she talks about it in detail in her book, *Mary Kay: You Can Have It All: Lifetime Wisdom from America's Foremost Woman Entrepreneur.* I put this strategy tip into action right from the beginning of my career in my home-based businesses, and that tip is the "six most important things to do list," which seems simple enough, but it truly makes a huge difference when put into action correctly, and I'm never going a day without it ever again. In a nut shell, every night I take the time to put together my six most important things list that I must get done the next day in my business. Not eight things or twenty things, but six—no more and no less. These are things that can only be done by me and not delegated to someone else; they are things that further my business and my cash flow. Yes, I have other lists that need to be done like errands, grocery lists, and such, but my six most important things to do list is my golden list that keeps me on task daily to generate new business, attend to current business, book more appointments, meet new people, sell more products and recruit new, effective team members. At the end of each day, whatever task was still on this list, if any, got put on the top of the list for the next day to be done first thing. Try this yourself for ninety days and let me know what results you experience. One hundred years ago, Charles Schwab was one of the smartest men of his day, and after ninety days of his top executives doing their list like this, he had such a massive increase in his company that he paid the man, Ivy Lee, $35,000 for giving him this idea, which was a lot of money back then when the average worker was earning only $2 a day. You can take this tip straight to the bank. Use it and let me know what happens to your business. Really, I want to hear from you!

Has being in your industry helped you to expand to other industries?

Absolutely yes, being a part of running my own home-based businesses has catapulted me into a thriving successful master coaching and speaking career known as Legacy Maker® Entrepreneur Coaching Systems. I do speak on many other topics and subjects as I'm in the media business as well, but the direct selling business was my launching pad to learning vital life, money, and business skills needed to becoming a professional coach, trainer, teacher, speaker, and mentor to so many others, and I love it so much. It's been life changing and priceless! Without experiencing success as an entrepreneur myself with all of life's ups, downs, twists, and turns, there would be no way I could stand on any stage and preach success. I have lived the life and can now turn around and bring others up with me because I have been in the trenches and won the battles, and the great news is, you can too!

If someone was to come to you for help, what would be the first thing you would tell them in regards to getting started in your industry?

I would ask them why they are thinking about joining the ranks of the direct selling industry. Knowing your why is the single most important thing to know when making this decision. The why can and does change over time, but knowing your why is most important to you right now; it matters immensely. When I got into direct sales for the very first time, I had two non-negotiable whys that mattered more to me than anything else, and they were my driving force when tough weeks came along and cancellations and objections became plentiful, which are all part of this business. Having a very strong reason why you are doing your business will get you through the toughest of times, and it must be a non-negotiable "why" as well. Failing to achieve your why is not an option in your book.

Outside of working (in your industry) what is your favorite thing to do?

My favorite thing to do is hosting my philanthropic Live Your Legacy Summits with my family, friends, and very special fans across the country. The summits teach people, especially women and teens, how to live their very best legacy right now despite whatever obstacles come their way. We also honor heroes who living their legacy out loud and helping others in a huge way either because of a tragedy in their life or simply because they feel called to action to be the person that helps others. They are true heroes in every sense of the word.

My summits are my babies, and I love them because they help so many people and bring such great people together in one room where amazing collaborations happen. Non-profits benefit greatly by being a big part of the guest list, and many times they are our honorees as well.

Many people, especially radio show hosts who have interviewed me over the years, ask me what I like to do in my quiet time, and I always have to chuckle to myself because quiet time is my least favorite thing in the world. My favorite pastime is being in a crowded room, using my God given voice that He restored to me after doctors said speaking aloud again would be impossible, to help others be the very best they can be and to help introduce them to their next best power partners in life, business, and even in their faith.

When I die, I want to be totally used up for God's purpose and have left no talent that He gave me untapped or unused for His glory and perfect will in my life and in others. So being with people, lots of people, is my favorite past time.

Do you provide coaching or resources to anyone who wants to further educate themselves in your industry?
Yes, I am an entrepreneur success coach who specializes in the direct sales home-based business industry. What my clients learn is massive but it is always completely customized to fit their wants, needs, and desired results at the part-time, full-time, or hobbyist level. I always want to help everyone rise to the top of their career path, but that is not always what they want for their own life and hectic schedules, as most people who join a home-based business do it part-time to simply earn a few extra dollars a month to supplement their family income, and

becoming a top performer and or leader in their company is not their goal.

So I pride myself on the fact that I listen intently to each person who comes to me wanting to know more about my coaching services, and I create all of their packages 100 percent designed to be a perfect fit for their life, their goals, and their specific financial desires. I never try and make people be or achieve something they are not comfortable being. Life is too short, so it has to be about being happy and fulfilled first and foremost, and the money will come if you love what you do and are not filled with stress that you unnecessarily put on yourself.

Is there anything you don't necessarily love about the industry?

Honestly the only thing I don't love about this industry is if and when I see a company compensation plan that is confusing, not very profitable for the sales force as they achieve higher level positions in it, and/or a very difficult compensation plan that the average consultant can't figure out easily and has no idea how to move up and give themselves a raise.

When a compensation plan is confusing to someone in the sales force, that means it is twice as confusing to explain to others who could be a potential new team member. An ill-constructed career plan can make or break a company, and I have seen several go out of business because of this very reason. Direct sales companies with an easy-to-follow, fast start program, and easy-to-understand compensation and advancement plans have a much higher success rate because a confused mind does nothing. Why companies find it hard to understand career plans is beyond me.

So many brand new independent sales people call me up wanting me to help them understand their own company's compensation plan, which is a red flag to me, and I can't help but to show them other companies with a better one in place to give them an idea of how it should be done, and then we dig into how theirs works. I even found a new direct sales company's compensation plan that gave their independent sales force less money when they achieved a very high position. The company wasn't even aware of that mistake on their end, and they quickly fixed the problem and were very happy I spotted that glitch in their career plan before anyone reached that level of success. Therefore, I highly recommend that before joining any company, you make sure moving up the compensation plan is simply laid out and easy to understand for you and your potential recruits.

What favorite marketing strategies have you used to help with building your business?
In person, online, and through networking groups and clubs are my three favorite ways to market my businesses.

My favorite strategy is old fashioned, in-person networking at local events that cater to my demographics—which in my case has always been women. Constantly searching and finding great events in your area to attend as a guest to mix and mingle with other like-minded people is a wonderful way to get to know your peers, learn from speakers, and build friendships in a fun atmosphere where you are not there to sell or recruit. This helps you build quality people in your life, and your relationship could become mutually beneficial to each other's businesses over time. Sometimes the connection and business sparks fly immediately when you meet, and other times there is a longer nurturing period before any business actually transpires. Sometimes you simply make a new friend, and that is great too. But no matter what happens, if you go to enough events every single month, you will become known for what you do, and that helps you with your brand recognition in your city and surrounding areas.

Next, your own social media business strategy is a must have these days, and if you have no idea what that looks like and how to rock the ever-changing social media world, then I highly suggest hiring a social media expert to at least get you started and set you up with a plan of action you can execute for yourself on a daily basis. You will probably meet many of them at local networking events. Having the right one on your staff will prove to be priceless to your business, your sales, your name recognition, and to so many more people finding you to buy your products and services and to join your team.

This is especially important in the home-based business arena because we have no territories, and the entire US is open game for you to sell to and recruit amazing new people from. Having your company's replicated website up and running in your name is not what I am talking about here. Your website will just sit there in cyber space with little or no traffic coming to it unless you have an aggressive social media marketing plan in action that tells the masses that your website is ready for them to buy from or to join your team from. Your strategy should also include you being an expert online in your field, giving of free knowledge, tips, and information on a regular basis to people who can and do follow you because they are interested in your topics. Your topics should have everything to do with your products and/or services, so these followers could potentially become your customers, clients, and/or team members. If you sell cosmetics, then doing your own how-to videos on glamor, style, fashion, makeup tips, and more should all be a part of your online presence. If you sell wellness or weight loss products, then videos, blogs, and posts on exercise, health alerts, and recipes could all be a part of your daily posts.

It always amazing me when direct sellers say these words: "I don't know anyone"—especially with the entire world at everyone's finger tips with the invention of smart phones. So find a way, make a way, or hire a way to get your social media income funnel stream live on the web to lead your ideal customers straight to your social media platforms and to your website right away. The world is waiting to meet you and what you have to offer.

Last, one of my favorite marketing strategies is being a very active member of the right clubs and networking groups where I can be of benefit to them as well as they being of support and benefit to me and what I have to offer. For example, I join wonderful women's groups like the Ewomen Network that has a flourishing chapter here in Atlanta where I live as well as a very large national membership that I can and do tap into in order to grow all of my businesses nationwide.

Knowing your ideal customer is also crucial when deciding which clubs to visit and/or join. You don't want to waste time and money in a room full of people that might have a 50/50 chance of needing or wanting your product or services. Instead, be very clear and specific on who you would like to service and get into their space often. If you're in the health and wellness industry don't just get into a room full of women in general; find the groups that cater to weight loss, or cancer survivors, or yoga enthusiasts, etc. Focusing in on a smaller demographic will give you better odds of meeting potential customers who are excited about what you sell. Other demographics will find you too, but spend most of your valuable time and money surrounding yourself with a specific type of person or persons on a regular basis.

If you are in the cosmetic business, why not choose a specific age range you want to cater to like teens or seniors or even young brides. You can focus each month or season on a different type of female, so you aren't just wandering around, looking for any woman with skin. Without targeting a specific group, the odds are against you before you even open your mouth. Don't be general; be selective in your search for new clients, customers and even team members.

Think of it this way, you go to school to become a doctor and you get your degree and PhD, but instead of being a general practitioner, you instead specialize in the heart. You're still a doctor, but you have selected a particular group of patients to cater to and with that, you become easier to find, and other doctors refer their patients to you as well. It is a winning combination. Be a specialist in your industry. It will pay off. Try it.

What are 3 books that you recommend for success in your industry?

- *I Won't Survive... I'll Thrive!* – Aurea McGarry
- *Rich Dad Poor Dad: What The Rich Teach Their Kids About Money That the Poor and Middle Class Do Not* – Robert Kiyosaki.
- *The 21 Irrefutable Laws Of Leadership* – John C. Maxwell

If there was one thing you may have done differently in your industry when you got started, what would it have been?

Hire a coach on day one who specialized in helping direct sellers treat their businesses like million dollar businesses to help set me up as the president of my own company. I would have saved years of trying to figure all of that out on my own and being subject to learning only what the people in my company taught me and my up line. Hiring an outside professional would have made a huge difference and I know that now because I am a coach. It was 2011 when I truly discovered the value of having my own personal business coach. Now, I always have a coach or two in my life at all times; they are priceless to me and my ongoing successes. All highly successful entrepreneurs have one or more in their lives too. Just ask them.

What is your favorite quote?

"Give your works wholly to the Lord and He will bless and prosper them." Proverbs 16:3

and also one of my original quotes with a little of my NYC humor

"If your ship doesn't come in, take a taxi!!!"

Special thanks to the following:

Dr. Matthew Boudreau
Chiropractor
Private practice
Facebook.com/resultsdc

Jasmine Thomas
Intern
Legacy Makers TV Show
Facebook.com/LegacyMakersTV

Eric Faltraco
President & CEO
Web, Graphic & Logo Design Company
Facebook.com/Eric.Faltraco

Dawn Brolin CPA,MSA
President & Founder
Powerful Accounting LLC.
AccountantFacebook.com/PowerfulAccounting

Tracy Sargent
Founder
K9 Search & Rescue Specialists
Facebook.com/Tracy.Sargent.562

Barbara Riley
Founder
The Amanda Riley Foundation
Facebook.com/AmandaRileyFoundation.Org

Mary Vidarte
Author & Speaker
PayDay 2 Profits
Facebook.com/Mary.Vidarte.9

Charlene McGregor
Sales Rep
Hegemon Group International
Facebook.com/Charlene.Mcgregor.9

Lori A. Manns
Founder & CEO
Quality Media Consultant Group
Facebook.com/QualityMediaConsultantGroup

Glenn Gordon
Inventor
We Gotcha Back - Orthopedic Back Belts
Facebook.com/Wgbbackbelt

Ires Alliston
Founder & CEO
Alliston Group LLC.
Facebook.com/AllistonGroup

Elisa Koning
Entrepreneur
The Selfie Station
Facebook.com/SelfieSocials05

Sandy Lomas
Founder & CEO
The Lomas List
Facebook.com/TheLomasList

Deborah Daniel CPA
President & Founder
Charter Accounting
Facebook.com/Deborah.Daniel.3538

Deidre Trudeau
Founder & President
Ezeeye Visual Brand & Graphics
Facebook.com/WomensSuccessNow

Beverly Bogus
Mortgage Broker
PCM Direct Mortgage
Facebook.com/Beverly.Bogus.5

Susan Smith
Fitteam Leader
Fitteam Global
Facebook.com/SusanRodgersSmith

Amanda Butler
Legal Shield Sales Rep
Legal Shield
Facebook.com/Amanda.Butler.9828

Conclusion

Congratulations as you have made it to the end of the book!

We hope this book has helped enlighten and teach you something new, and we wish you the very best in all your endeavors. We know that you are now equipped with proper information to get you started on your path to multiple streams of income.

Now that you have read this book, we hope that you have been inspired to add additional streams of income to your life. It's a must to continue survive in the future. We encourage you to reach out to one or many of our authors. Connect with them on social media and find out how you can work with them directly. Also be sure to let us know what you enjoyed most about this book and leave your rating on Amazon. It would be so appreciated. In fact, if you do leave your rating on Amazon, be sure to include your email for a free gift.

If you would like to know how you can be a part of the next edition, be sure to visit our website www.MultipleStreamsofIncomeBook.com. Our goal is to come out with a new edition every six to twelve months to help bring more education, empowerment, and inspiration to women and men all over the world. Also be sure to pay close attention to the Show Your Success Dinner and MSOI workshop where you will get hands-on education from our authors to learn more in depth of how you too can bring in multiple streams of income into your home.

We wish you much success!

Made in the USA
Monee, IL
28 March 2022

93704016R00105